McDougal Littell
Algebra 1
Concepts and Skills

Larson   Boswell   Kanold   Stiff

Practice Workbook
with Examples

The Practice Workbook provides additional practice with worked-out examples for every lesson. The workbook covers essential skills and vocabulary. Space is provided for students to show their work.

McDougal Littell
A HOUGHTON MIFFLIN COMPANY

Evanston, Illinois · Boston · Dallas

Contents

Algebra 1. Concepts and Skills
Practice Workbook with Examples

NAME _____ DATE _____

Practice with Examples

For use with pages 3–8

GOAL **Evaluate variable expressions.**

> **VOCABULARY**
>
> A **variable** is a letter that is used to represent a range of numbers.
>
> A **variable expression** consists of constants, variables, and operations.
>
> To evaluate a variable expression, you write the expression, substitute the given number for each variable, and simplify.

EXAMPLE 1 *Describe a Variable Expression*

Variable Expression	Meaning	Operation
$3x$, $3 \cdot x$, $(3)(x)$	3 times x	Multiplication
$\dfrac{3}{x}$, $3 \div x$	3 divided by x	Division
$3 + x$	3 plus x	Addition
$3 - x$	3 minus x	Subtraction

Exercises for Example 1

State the meaning of the variable expression and name the operation.

1. $4 - x$

2. $7y$

3. $x + 1$

4. $\dfrac{y}{2}$

EXAMPLE 2 *Evaluate a Variable Expression*

Evaluate the expression when $y = 3$.

a. $y - 1$

b. $12y$

SOLUTION

a. $y - 1 = 3 - 1$ Substitute 3 for y.

        $= 2$ Simplify.

b. $12y = 12(3)$ Substitute 3 for y.

        $= 36$ Simplify.

Algebra 1, Concepts and Skills
Practice Workbook with Examples

NAME _____ DATE _____

Practice with Examples

For use with pages 3–8

Exercises for Example 2

Evaluate the expression for the given value of the variable.

5. $8 + x$ when $x = 6$

6. $\dfrac{10}{s}$ when $s = 2$

7. a when $a = 20$

8. $9 - y$ when $y = 1$

9. $9q$ when $q = 12$

10. $8b$ when $b = 3$

EXAMPLE 3 *Evaluate d = rt to Find Distance*

Find the distance d traveled if you drive at an average speed of 65 miles per hour for 5 hours.

SOLUTION

$d = rt$	Write formula.
$= 65(5)$	Substitute 65 for r and 5 for t.
$= 325$	Simplify.

The distance traveled is 325 miles.

Exercises for Example 3

11. Find the distance traveled if you drive at an average speed of 60 miles per hour for 4 hours.

12. Find the distance traveled by an airplane flying at an average speed of 350 miles per hour for 6 hours.

Practice with Examples

For use with pages 3–8

EXAMPLE 4 *Finding Area and Perimeter*

a. The area A of a triangle is equal to half the base b times the height h:

$A = \frac{1}{2}bh$. Find the area of the triangle below in square feet.

b. The perimeter P of a triangle is equal to the sum of the lengths of its sides:
$P = a + b + c$. Find the perimeter of the triangle below in feet.

SOLUTION

a. $A = \frac{1}{2}bh$ Write formula.

$A = \frac{1}{2}(4)(3)$ Substitute 4 for b and 3 for h.

$A = 6$ Simplify.

The triangle has an area of 6 square feet.

b. $P = a + b + c$ Write formula.

$P = 3 + 4 + 5$ Substitute 4 for b and 3 for h.

$P = 12$ Simplify.

The triangle has a perimeter of 12 feet.

Exercises for Example 4

13. Find the area of a triangle with a base of 10 inches and a height of 6 inches.

14. Find the perimeter of a triangle with side lengths 3 inches, 9 inches, and 11 inches.

Practice with Examples

For use with pages 9–14

GOAL **Evaluate a power.**

> ### VOCABULARY
>
> An expression like 2^3 is called a **power,** where the **exponent** 3 represents the number of times the **base** 2 is used as a factor.
>
> **Grouping symbols,** such as parentheses or brackets, indicate the order in which operations should be performed.

EXAMPLE 1 *Read and Write Powers*

Express the power in words. Then write the meaning.

Exponential Form	Word	Meaning
a. 2^4	two to the fourth power	$2 \cdot 2 \cdot 2 \cdot 2$
b. x^2	x squared	$x \cdot x$

Exercises for Example 1

Express the power in words. Then write the meaning.

  1. 3^3

  2. 5^2

  3. x^3

EXAMPLE 2 *Evaluate Powers*

Evaluate the expression y^4 when $y = 3$.

SOLUTION

$$y^4 = 3^4 \qquad \text{Substitute 3 for } y.$$
$$= 3 \cdot 3 \cdot 3 \cdot 3 \qquad \text{Write factors.}$$
$$= 81 \qquad \text{Multiply.}$$

The value of the expression is 81.

Algebra 1, Concepts and Skills
Practice Workbook with Examples

Practice with Examples

For use with pages 9–14

Exercises for Example 2

Evaluate the expression for the given value of the variable.

4. q^3 when $q = 10$

5. b^5 when $b = 2$

6. z^2 when $z = 5$

7. x^4 when $x = 6$

8. m^3 when $m = 9$

9. n^5 when $n = 3$

EXAMPLE 3 *Exponents and Grouping Symbols*

Evaluate the expression when $x = 2$.

a. $3x^4$

b. $(3x)^4$

SOLUTION

a. $3x^4 = 3(2^4)$ Substitute 2 for x.

$= 3(16)$ Evaluate power.

$= 48$ Multiply.

Exercises for Example 3

Evaluate the expression for the given values of the variables.

10. $(c + d)^3$ when $c = 2$ and $d = 5$

11. $c^3 + d^3$ when $c = 2$ and $d = 5$

12. $5p^2$ when $p = 2$

13. $(5p)^2$ when $p = 2$

Practice with Examples

For use with pages 9–14

EXAMPLE 4 *Find Volume*

A storage crate has the shape of a cube. Each edge of the crate is 5 feet long. Find the volume of the crate in cubic feet.

SOLUTION

$V = s^3$ Write formula for volume.

$\quad = 5^3$ Substitute 5 for s.

$\quad = 125$ Evaluate power.

The volume of the storage crate is 125 ft^3.

Exercises for Example 4

14. The formula for the area of a square is $A = s^2$.
Find the area of a square when $s = 10$ ft.

15. The formula for the area of a square is $A = s^2$.
Find the area of a square when $s = 12$ cm.

LESSON 1.3

Practice with Examples

For use with pages 15–21

GOAL Use the established order of operations.

> ### VOCABULARY
>
> An established **order of operations** is used to evaluate an expression involving more than one operation.

EXAMPLE 1 *Evaluate Expressions Without Grouping Symbols*

---

a. Evaluate $5x^2 - 6$ when $x = 3$. Use the order of operations.

b. Evaluate $7 + 15 \div 3 - 4$. Use the order of operations.

SOLUTION

a. $5x^2 - 6 = 5 \cdot 3^2 - 6$ Substitute 3 for x.

$ = 5 \cdot 9 - 6$ Evaluate power.

$ = 45 - 6$ Evaluate product.

$ = 39$ Evaluate difference.

b. $7 + 15 \div 3 - 4 = 7 + (15 \div 3) - 4$ Divide first.

$ = 7 + 5 - 4$ Evaluate quotient.

$ = 12 - 4$ Work from left to right.

$ = 8$ Evaluate difference.

Exercises for Example 1

Evaluate the expression.

1. $4 \cdot 3 + 8 \div 2$

2. $24 \div 6 \cdot 2$

3. $21 - 5 \cdot 2$

Practice with Examples

For use with pages 15–21

EXAMPLE 2 *Evaluate Expressions With Grouping Symbols*

Evaluate $24 \div (6 \cdot 2)$. Use the order of operations.

SOLUTION

$$24 \div (6 \cdot 2) = 24 \div 12 \qquad \text{Simplify } 6 \cdot 2.$$
$$= 2 \qquad \text{Evaluate the quotient.}$$

Exercises for Example 2

Evaluate the expression.

4. $(6 - 2)^2 - 1$

5. $30 \div (1 + 4) + 2$

6. $(8 + 4) \div (1 + 2) + 1$

7. $6 - (2^2 - 1)$

8. $(30 \div 1) + (4 + 2)$

9. $8 + 4 \div (1 + 2 + 1)$

Algebra 1, Concepts and Skills
Practice Workbook with Examples

NAME _____ DATE _____

Practice with Examples

For use with pages 15–21

EXAMPLE 3 *Calculate Family Admission Prices*

Use the table below which shows admission prices for a theme park. Suppose a family of 2 adults and 3 children go to the park. The children's ages are 6 years, 8 years, and 13 years.

a. Write an expression that represents the admission price for the family.

b. Use a calculator to evaluate the expression.

Theme Park Admission Prices	
Age	*Admission Price*
Adults	$34.00
Children (3–9 years)	$21.00
Children (2 years and under)	free

SOLUTION

a. The admission price for the child who is 13 years old is $34, the adult price. The family must buy 3 adult tickets and 2 children's tickets. An expression that represents the admission price for the family is $3(34) + 2(21)$.

b. If your calculator uses the established order of operations, the following keystroke sequence gives the result 144.

3 $\times$ 34 $+$ 2 $\times$ 21 ENTER

The admission price for the family is $144.

Exercise for Example 3

10. Rework Example 3 for a family of 2 adults and 4 children. The children's ages are 2 years, 4 years, 10 years, and 12 years.

NAME _____ DATE _____

Practice with Examples

For use with pages 22–29

GOAL **Check solutions of equations and inequalities.**

> **VOCABULARY**
>
> An **equation** is a statement formed when an equal sign is placed between two expressions.
>
> When the variable in an equation is replaced by a number and the resulting statement is true, the number is a **solution of the equation.**
>
> Finding all the solutions of an equation is called **solving the equation.**
>
> An **inequality** is a statement formed when an inequality symbol is placed between two expressions.
>
> A **solution of an inequality** is a number that produces a true statement when it is substituted for the variable in the inequality.

EXAMPLE 1 *Check Possible Solutions of an Equation*

Check whether the numbers 2 and 4 are solutions of the equation
$2x + 3 = 11$

SOLUTION

To check the possible solutions, substitute them into the equation. If both sides of the equation have the same value, then the number is a solution.

x	$2x + 3 = 11$	Result	Conclusion
2	$2(2) + 3 \stackrel{?}{=} 11$	$7 \neq 11$	2 is not a solution
4	$2(4) + 3 \stackrel{?}{=} 11$	$11 = 11$	4 is a solution

The number 4 is a solution of $2x + 3 = 11$. The number 2 is not a solution.

Exercises for Example 1
Check whether the given number is a solution of the equation.

1. $5p - 2 = 12; 3$

2. $8 + 2y = 10; 3$

3. $3a + 2 = 14; 2$

4. $\dfrac{t}{4} - 3 = 0; 12$

5. $n + 4n = 20; 5$

6. $k + 7 = 3k + 1; 3$

NAME _____ DATE _____

Practice with Examples

For use with pages 22–29

EXAMPLE 2 *Use Mental Math to Solve an Equation*

Which question could be used to find the solution of the equation $x - 7 = 15$?

A. What number can be subtracted from 7 to get 15?

B. What number can 7 be subtracted from to get 15?

C. What number can 15 be subtracted from to get 7?

SOLUTION

Because 7 can be subtracted from 22 to get 15, question B could be used to solve the equation $x - 7 = 15$.

Exercises for Example 2

Write a question that could be used to solve the equation. Then use mental math to solve the equation.

7. $x + 7 = 21$

8. $3f + 1 = 19$

9. $a - 12 = 10$

10. $\dfrac{y}{3} = 11$

11. $4j - 7 = 9$

12. $\dfrac{b}{2} = 4$

Practice with Examples

For use with pages 22–29

EXAMPLE 3 *Check Solutions of Inequalities*

Decide whether 6 is a solution of the inequality.

a. $3 + w \geq 9$ **b.** $r + 4 > 11$

SOLUTION

Inequality	Substitution	Result	Conclusion
a. $3 + w \geq 9$	$3 + 6 \overset{?}{\geq} 9$	$9 \geq 9$	6 is a solution.
b. $r + 4 > 11$	$6 + 4 \overset{?}{>} 11$	$10 \not> 11$	6 is not a solution.

Exercises for Example 3

Check whether the given number is a solution of the inequality.

13. $2f - 3 \geq 8; \ 5$

14. $2h - 4 > 10; \ 3$

15. $13x \leq 6x + 15; \ 2$

NAME _____ DATE _____

Practice with Examples

For use with pages 30–35

GOAL **Translate words into mathematical symbols.**

> ### VOCABULARY
>
> In order to solve real-life problems, you will **translate** words into mathematical symbols. In English, phrases are not complete sentences. In math, **phrases** are translated into variable expressions. Sentences are translated into equations or inequalities.

EXAMPLE 1 *Translate Addition and Subtraction Phrases*

Write the phrase as a variable expression. Let x represent the number.

Phrase	Translation
a. The sum of 3 and a number	$3 + x$
b. The difference between a number and 4	$x - 4$
c. 15 more than a number	$15 + x$
d. A number decreased by 7	$x - 7$

Exercises for Example 1

Write the phrase as a variable expression. Let *x* represent the number.

1. The sum of 1 and a number

2. 4 less than a number

3. 12 minus a number

4. A number plus 8

5. A number increased by 6

6. The difference between a number and 10

Algebra 1, Concepts and Skills
Practice Workbook with Examples

NAME _____ DATE _____

Practice with Examples

For use with pages 30–35

EXAMPLE 2 **Translate Multiplication and Division Phrases**

Write the phrase as a variable expression. Let *n* represent the number.

Phrase	Translation
a. 8 times a number	$8n$
b. The quotient of a number and 2	$\dfrac{n}{2}$
c. A number multiplied by 4	$4n$

Exercises for Example 2

Write the phrase as a variable expression. Let *n* represent the number.

7. The product of 3 and a number

8. The quotient of a number and 4

9. 12 multiplied by a number

10. One half of a number

11. 9 divided by a number

NAME _____ DATE _____

Practice with Examples

For use with pages 30–35

EXAMPLE 3 **Write and Solve an Equation**

a. Translate into mathematical symbols: "The product of a number and 8 is 56." Let x represent the number.

b. Use mental math to solve your equation and check your solution.

SOLUTION

a. The equation is $8x = 56$.

b. Using mental math, the solution is $x = 7$.

$$8 \cdot x = 56$$
$$8 \cdot 7 = 56$$
$$56 = 56$$

Exercises for Example 3

Translate each sentence into mathematical symbols. Then use mental math to solve your equation. Let *x* represent the number.

12. A number plus 6 is 15.

13. The quotient of a number and 4 is 7.

14. A number increased by 8 is 15.

15. A number multiplied by 3 is 33.

Algebra 1, Concepts and Skills
Practice Workbook with Examples

Practice with Examples

For use with pages 36–41

GOAL **Model and solve real-life problems.**

> ### VOCABULARY
>
> Writing algebraic expressions, equations, or inequalities that represent real-life situations is called **modeling**. First you write a **verbal model** using words. Then you translate the verbal model into an **algebraic model**.

EXAMPLE 1 *Write an Algebraic Model*

A movie theater charges $6 admission. The total sales on a given day were $420. How many admission tickets were sold that day?

SOLUTION

Verbal Model

$$\boxed{\text{Cost per Ticket}} \cdot \boxed{\text{Number of tickets}} = \boxed{\text{Total sales}}$$

Labels

Cost per ticket = 6   (dollars)

Number of tickets = n (tickets)

Total sales = 420   (dollars)

Algebraic Model

$6n = 420$ Write algebraic model.

$n = 70$ Solve using mental math.

The number of tickets sold is 70.

Practice with Examples

For use with pages 36–41

Exercises for Example 1

In Exercises 1 and 2, do the following.

  a. Write a verbal model.

  b. Assign labels and write an algebraic model based on your verbal model.

  c. Use mental math to solve the equation.

1. The student government is selling baseball hats at $8 each. The group wants to raise $2480. How many hats does the group need to sell?

2. You and your two sisters bought a gift for your brother. You paid $7.50 for your share (one-third of the gift). What was the total cost of the gift?

Practice with Examples

For use with pages 36–41

EXAMPLE 2 *Write an Algebraic Model*

You are hiking on a trail. You hike at an average speed of 1.5 miles per hour for 2.8 miles. During the last 3.4 miles, you increase your average speed by 0.2 miles per hour. How long will it take you to walk the last 3.4 miles?

SOLUTION

| **Verbal Model** | $\left(\boxed{\text{Speed for first 2.8 miles}} + 0.2 \right) \cdot \boxed{\text{Time}} = \boxed{\text{Distance}}$ |

Labels Speed for first 2.8 miles = 1.5 (miles per hour)

Time = x (hours)

Distance = 3.4 (miles)

Algebraic Model

$(1.5 + 0.2) \cdot (x) = 3.4$ Write algebraic model.

$1.7x = 3.4$ Simplify.

$x = 2$ Solve using mental math.

It will take 2 hours.

Exercises for Example 2

3. A car travels at an average speed of 45 miles per hour for 8 miles, reduces its speed by 15 miles per hour for the next 4 miles, and then returns to a speed of 45 miles per hour. How long does the car travel at the reduced speed?

NAME _____ DATE _____

Practice with Examples

For use with pages 42–47

GOAL Organize data using a table or graph

> ## VOCABULARY
>
> **Data** are information, facts, or numbers that describe something.
>
> **Bar graphs** and **line graphs** are used to organize data.

EXAMPLE 1 *Organize Data in a Table*

The data in the table show the number of passenger cars produced by three automobile manufacturers.

Passenger Car Production (in thousands)						
Year	**1970**	**1975**	**1980**	**1985**	**1990**	**1995**
Company A	1273	903	639	1266	727	577
Company B	2017	1808	1307	1636	1377	1396
Company C	2979	3679	4065	4887	2755	2515

a. During what year was the total passenger car production the highest?

b. During what year was the total passenger car production the lowest?

SOLUTION

Add another row to the table. Enter the total passenger car production of all three companies.

Year	**1970**	**1975**	**1980**	**1985**	**1990**	**1995**
Total	6269	6390	6011	7789	4859	4488

a. From the table, you can see that the total passenger car production was the highest in 1985.

b. From the table, you can see that the total passenger car production was the lowest in 1995.

Exercises for Example 1

In Exercises 1 and 2, use the data from Example 1.

1. During what year was the total passenger car production by Company B the highest?

2. During what year was the total passenger car production by Company C the lowest?

Practice with Examples

For use with pages 42–47

EXAMPLE 2 *Make and Interpret a Line Graph*

Use the data from Example 1. Draw a line graph to organize the data for Company A's passenger car production.

a. During which 5-year period did Company A's passenger car production decrease the least?

b. During which 5-year period did Company A's passenger car production decrease the most?

SOLUTION

Draw the vertical scale from 0 to 1400 thousand cars in increments of 200 thousand cars. Mark the number of years on the horizontal axis starting with 1970. For each number of passenger cars produced, draw a point on the graph. Then draw a line from each point to the next point.

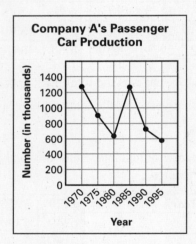

**Company A's Passenger
Car Production**

a. Company A's passenger car production decreased the least from 1990–1995.

b. Company A's passenger car production decreased the most from 1985–1990.

Algebra 1, Concepts and Skills
Practice Workbook with Examples

Practice with Examples

For use with pages 42–47

Exercises for Example 2

In Exercises 3 and 4, use the data from Example 1.

3. Draw a line graph to organize the data for Company C's passenger car production. During which 5-year period did Company C's passenger car production decrease the most?

4. Draw a line graph to organize the data for Company B's passenger car production. During which 5-year period did Company B's passenger car production increase the most?

Algebra 1, Concepts and Skills
Practice Workbook with Examples

Practice with Examples

For use with pages 48–54

GOAL **Use four differrent ways to represent functions.**

> ## VOCABULARY
>
> A **function** is a rule that establishes a relationship between two quanti-
> ties, called the **input** and the **output.**
>
> Making an **input-output table** is one way to describe a function.
>
> The collection of all input values is the **domain** of the function.
>
> The collection of all output values is the **range** of the function.

EXAMPLE 1 *Identify a Function*

Does the table represent a function? Explain.

Input	Output
5	1
5	2
10	3
15	4

SOLUTION

The table does not represent a function. For the input value 5, there are
two output values, not one.

Exercises for Example 1

**In Exercises 1 and 2, does the table represent a function?
Explain.**

1.

Input	Output
1	4
2	8
3	12
4	16

2.

Input	Output
1	5
2	6
2	7
3	8

NAME _____ DATE _____

Practice with Examples

For use with pages 48–54

EXAMPLE 2 *Make an Input-Output Table*

Make an input-output table for the function $y = 3x + 1.5$. Use 0, 1, 2, and 3 as the domain.

SOLUTION

List an output for each of the inputs.

INPUT	FUNCTION	OUTPUT
$x = 0$	$y = 3(0) + 1.5$	$y = 1.5$
$x = 1$	$y = 3(1) + 1.5$	$y = 4.5$
$x = 2$	$y = 3(2) + 1.5$	$y = 7.5$
$x = 3$	$y = 3(3) + 1.5$	$y = 10.5$

Make an input-output table.

Input x	Output y
0	1.5
1	4.5
2	7.5
3	10.5

Exercises for Example 2

In Exercises 3–5, make an input-output table for the function. Use 0, 1, 2, and 3 as the domain.

3. $y = 5 - x$

4. $y = 4x + 1$

5. $y = 9 - x$

Algebra 1, Concepts and Skills
Practice Workbook with Examples

Practice with Examples

For use with pages 48–54

EXAMPLE 3 *Write an Equation*

The county fair charges $4 per vehicle and $1.50 for each person in the vehicle. Represent the total charge C as a function of the number of persons p. Write an equation for the function.

SOLUTION

Verbal Model

Total charge	=	Vehicle charge	+	Rate per person	·	Number of persons

Labels Total charge $= C$ (dollars)
Vehicle charge $= 4$ (dollars)
Rate per person $= 1.50$ (dollars)
Number of persons $= p$ (persons)

Algebraic Model $C = 4 + 1.5p$

Exercises for Example 3

6. Rework Example 3 if the vehicle charge is $1.50 and $4 is charged for each person in the vehicle.

7. Rework Example 3 if the vehicle charge is $3 and $2.50 is charged for each person in the vehicle.

NAME _____ DATE _____

Practice with Examples

For use with pages 65–70

GOAL Graph, compare, and order real numbers.

VOCABULARY

Real numbers are the positive numbers, the negative numbers, and zero.

The **real number line** is a line whose points correspond to the real numbers.

Negative numbers are numbers less than zero.

Positive numbers are numbers greater than zero.

Integers are the numbers …, −3, −2, −1, 0, 1, 2, 3 … .

Whole numbers are the positive integers and zero.

The **graph** of a number is the point that corresponds to the number.

EXAMPLE 1 *Graphing and Comparing Integers*

Graph −3 and 2 on a number line. Then write two inequalities that compare the two numbers.

SOLUTION

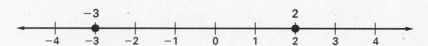

On the graph, −3 is to the left of 2, so −3 is less than 2. You can write this using the symbols:

$$-3 < 2$$

On the graph, 2 is to the right of −3, so 2 is greater than −3. You can write this using the symbols:

$$2 > -3$$

Exercises for Example 1
....

Graph the numbers on a number line. Then write two inequalities that compare the numbers.

1. −4 and −7   **2.** −8 and 9   **3.** 5 and −6

Algebra 1, Concepts and Skills
Practice Workbook with Examples

NAME _____ DATE _____

Practice with Examples

For use with pages 65–70

EXAMPLE 2 *Graphing Real Numbers*

Graph −1.5 and 1.0 on a number line. Then write two inequalities that compare the two numbers.

SOLUTION

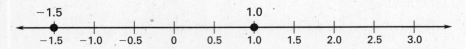

On the graph, −1.5 is to the left of 1.0, so −1.5 is less than 1.0.

$$-1.5 < 1.0$$

On the graph, 1.0 is to the right of −1.5, so 1.0 is greater than −1.5

$$1.0 > -1.5$$

Exercises for Example 2

Graph the numbers on a number line. Then write two inequalities that compare the two numbers.

4. −2.3 and −2.8

5. −5.2 and −4.8

6. −0.6 and 0.3

Algebra 1, Concepts and Skills
Practice Workbook with Examples

NAME _____ DATE _____

Practice with Examples

For use with pages 65–70

EXAMPLE 3 **Ordering Real Numbers**

Write the following numbers in increasing order: $3.5, -3, 0, -1.5, -0.2, 2$.

SOLUTION

First graph the numbers on a number line.

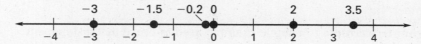

From the graph, you can see that the order is $-3, -1.5, -0.2, 0, 2, 3.5$.

Exercises for Example 3

Write the numbers in increasing order.

7. $2, -3, -2.5, 4.5, -1.5$

8. $-\frac{3}{4}, \frac{1}{4}, -2, -\frac{5}{4}, 1$

NAME _____ DATE _____

Practice with Examples

For use with pages 71–76

GOAL **Find the opposite and absolute value of a number.**

VOCABULARY

Opposites are two numbers that are the same distance from zero on a number line but on opposite sides.

The **absolute value** of a real number is its distance from zero on a number line.

A **counterexample** is a single example used to prove that a statement is false.

EXAMPLE 1 *Finding the Opposite and the Absolute Value of a Number*

a. Find the opposite of each of the numbers 3.6 and −7.

b. Find the absolute value of each of the numbers 3.6 and −7.

SOLUTION

a. The opposite of 3.6 is −3.6 because each is 3.6 units from zero. The opposite of −7 is 7 because each is 7 units from zero.

b. The absolute value of 3.6 is 3.6. The absolute value of −7 is 7 because the absolute value of a number represents distance, which is never negative.

Exercises for Example 1

Find the opposite of the number. Then find the absolute value of the number.

1. −1.7   **2.** 4.2   **3.** −5

Practice with Examples

For use with pages 71–76

EXAMPLE 2 *Solve an Absolute Value Equation*

Use mental math to solve the equation. If there is no solution, write *no solution.*

a. $|x| = 3$ **b.** $|x| = -0.5$ **c.** $|x| = \dfrac{1}{3}$

SOLUTIONS

a. $-3, 3$ **b.** no solution   **c.** $-\dfrac{1}{3}, \dfrac{1}{3}$

Exercises for Example 2

Use mental math to solve the equation. If there is no solution, write *no solution.*

4. $|x| = 1.8$ **5.** $|x| = -14$ **6.** $|x| = 11.3$

EXAMPLE 3 *Finding Velocity and Speed*

An elevator descends at a rate of 900 feet per minute. Find the velocity and the speed of the elevator.

SOLUTION

Velocity $= -900$ ft per min   Motion is downward.

Speed $= |-900| = 900$ ft per min   Speed is positive.

Exercises for Example 3

Find the speed and the velocity of the object.

7. A duck hawk descends at 150 miles per hour when striking its prey.

8. A helicopter descends at a rate of 8 feet per second.

Algebra 1, Concepts and Skills
Practice Workbook with Examples

Practice with Examples

For use with pages 71–76

EXAMPLE 4 *Use a Counterexample*

Determine whether the statement is *true* or *false*. If it is false, give a counterexample.

a. The quotient of a number and its opposite is always equal to 1.

b. The expression $\dfrac{|a|}{a}$ is always equal to -1.

SOLUTION

a. False. Counterexample: $\dfrac{5}{-5} = -1$

b. False. Counterexample: If $a = 5$, then $\dfrac{|5|}{5} = \dfrac{5}{5} = 1$.

Exercises for Example 4

Determine whether the statement is true or false. If it is false, give a counterexample.

9. The sum of a number and its opposite is always 0.

10. The product of a number and its opposite is always negative.

11. The absolute value of a negative fraction is always greater than 1.

NAME _____ DATE _____

Practice with Examples

For use with pages 77–83

GOAL Add real numbers using a number line or the rules of addition.

VOCABULARY

Closure property The sum of any two real numbers is a unique real number. $a + b$ is a real unique number.

Commutative property The order in which two numbers are added does not chance the sum. $a + b = b + a$.

Associative property The way three numbers are grouped when adding does not change the sum. $(a + b) + c = a + (b + c)$

Identity property The sum of a number and 0 is the number. $a + 0 = a$

Inverse property The sum of a number and its opposite is 0. $a + (-a) = 0$

EXAMPLE 1 *Adding Real Numbers*

Use a number line to find the sum: $4 + 1 + (-3)$.

SOLUTION

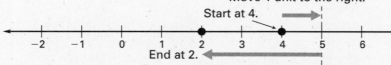

The sum can be written as $4 + 1 + (-3) = 2$.

Exercises for Example 1

Use a number line to find the sum.

1. $-8 + 6$

2. $-5 + (-1)$

3. $10 + (-4)$

4. $9 + (-3) + (-2)$

5. $-2 + (-4) + (-1)$

6. $6 + 1 + (-7)$

Practice with Examples

For use with pages 77–83

EXAMPLE 2 *Using Rules and Properties of Addition to Find a Sum*

Find the sum: $3.8 + (-1.2) + 1.2$.

SOLUTION

$$3.8 + (-1.2) + 1.2 = 3.8 + (-1.2 + 1.2) \qquad \text{Use associative property.}$$
$$= 3.8 + 0 \qquad \text{Use inverse property.}$$
$$= 3.8 \qquad \text{Use identity property.}$$

Exercises for Example 2

Name the property shown by the statement.

7. $(-6) + (-7) = (-7) + (-6)$ **8.** $5 + 0 = 5$

9. $(-4 + 8) + 6 = -4 + (8 + 6)$ **10.** $13 + (-13) = 0$

Algebra 1, Concepts and Skills
Practice Workbook with Examples

NAME _____ DATE _____

Practice with Examples

For use with pages 77–83

EXAMPLE 3 *Using Addition in Real Life*

The temperature rose 5°F from 7 A.M. to 11 A.M., rose 2°F from 11 A.M. to 5 P.M., and then fell 6°F from 5 P.M. to 10 P.M.

Use the properties of addition and the rules of addition to find the overall change in temperature.

SOLUTION

The overall change in temperature is represented as $5 + 2 + (-6)$.

$$5 + 2 + (-6) = (5 + 2) + (-6) \qquad \text{Use associative property.}$$
$$= 7 + (-6) \qquad \text{Add 5 and 2.}$$
$$= 1 \qquad \text{Add 7 and } -6.$$

The overall change in temperature, a rise, can be written as 1°F.

Exercises for Example 3

11. A bookstore had a first-quarter profit of $342.60, a second-quarter loss of $78.35, a third-quarter loss of $127.40, and a fourth-quarter profit of $457.80. Did the store make a profit during the year? Explain.

12. The price of a share of stock increased $3.00 on Monday, decreased $1.25 on Wednesday, and decreased $2.00 on Friday. Find the overall change in the price of a share of the stock.

NAME _____ DATE _____

Practice with Examples

For use with pages 84–91

GOAL Subtract real numbers using the subtraction rule.

> **VOCABULARY**
>
> The **terms** of an expression are the parts that are added when the expression is written as a sum.

EXAMPLE 1 *Using the Subtraction Rule*

Find the difference.

a. $-2 - 6$ **b.** $-1 - (-9)$

SOLUTION

a. $-2 - 6 = -2 + (-6)$ Add the opposite of 6.

            $= -8$ Add -2 and -6.

b. $-1 - (-9) = -1 + 9$ Add the opposite of -9.

               $= 8$ Add -1 and 9.

Exercises for Example 1

Find the difference.

1. $2 - 5$ **2.** $-5 - 7$ **3.** $2.5 - 4$

4. $4 - 2.5$ **5.** $10 - 2$ **6.** $10 - (-2)$

NAME _____ DATE _____

Practice with Examples

For use with pages 84–91

EXAMPLE 2 *Evaluating Expressions*

Evaluate the expression $-8 - 3 - (-10) + 2$.

SOLUTION

$$
\begin{aligned}
-8 - 3 - (-10) + 2 &= -8 + (-3) + 10 + 2 && \text{Add the opposites of 3 and } -10. \\
&= -11 + 10 + 2 && \text{Add } -8 \text{ and } -3. \\
&= -1 + 2 && \text{Add } -11 \text{ and } 10. \\
&= 1 && \text{Add } -1 \text{ and } 2.
\end{aligned}
$$

Exercises for Example 2

Evaluate the expression.

7. $5 + (-3) - 1$ **8.** $9 - (-2) + 7$ **9.** $-6 - 2 + (-5)$

EXAMPLE 3 *Finding the Terms of an Expression*

Find the terms of $-8 - 3x$.

SOLUTION

$$-8 - 3x = -8 + (-3x) \qquad \text{Rewrite the difference as a sum.}$$

When an expression is written as a sum, the parts that are added are the terms of the expression. The terms of the expression are -8 and $-3x$.

Exercises for Example 3.

Find the terms of the expression.

10. $7 - 4x$ **11.** $-y - 5$ **12.** $-2a + 1$

NAME _____ DATE _____

Practice with Examples

For use with pages 84–91

EXAMPLE 4 *Using Subtraction in Real Life*

You record the daily high temperature for one week. The temperatures (in degrees Fahrenheit) are given in the table. Find the change in the temperature from each day to the next to complete the table.

Day	Sun	Mon	Tue	Wed	Thu	Fri	Sat
High Temperature	72	75	70	67	71	72	68
Change	—	?	?	?	?	?	?

SOLUTION

Subtract each day's temperature from the temperature for the previous day.

DAY	HIGH TEMPERATURE	CHANGE
Sun	72	—
Mon	75	$75 - 72 = 3$
Tue	70	$70 - 75 = -5$
Wed	67	$67 - 70 = -3$
Thu	71	$71 - 67 = 4$
Fri	72	$72 - 71 = 1$
Sat	68	$68 - 72 = -4$

Exercise for Example 4

13. The amount of snowfall is recorded for each week in the month of January. The amounts (in inches) are given in the table. Find the change in the amount of snowfall from each week to the next to complete the table.

Week	1	2	3	4
Amount	9	6.5	11	14
Change	—	?	?	?

Algebra 1, Concepts and Skills
Practice Workbook with Examples

Practice with Examples

For use with pages 92–98

GOAL Multiply real numbers using the rules for the sign of a product.

VOCABULARY

Closure property The product of any two real numbers is a unique real number. *ab* is a unique real number.

Commutative property The order in which two numbers are multiplied does not change the product. $ab = ba$

Associative property The way three numbers are grouped when multiplying does not change the product. $(ab)c = a(bc)$

Identity property The product of a number and 1 is the number.
$1 \cdot a = a$

Property of zero The product of a number and 0 is 0. $0 \cdot a = 0$

Property of negative 1 The product of a number and -1 is the opposite of the number. $-1 \cdot a = -a$

EXAMPLE 1 *Multiplying Real Numbers*

Find the product.

   a. $(0.5)(-26)$

   b. $(-1)(-5)(-6)$

   c. $(-4)(6)\left(-\frac{1}{3}\right)$

SOLUTION

   a. $(0.5)(-26) = -13$ One negative factor

   b. $(-1)(-5)(-6) = -30$ Three negative factors

   c. $(-4)(6)\left(-\frac{1}{3}\right) = 8$ Two negative factors

---

Exercises for Example 1

Find the product.

   1. $(-2)(3)$ **2.** $(-7)(-1)$ **3.** $(10)(-2)$

   4. $(-12)(0.5)(-3)$ **5.** $(-4)(-2)(-5)$ **6.** $(6)(-6)(2)$

Practice with Examples

For use with pages 92–98

EXAMPLE 2 *Simplifying Variable Expressions*

Simplify the expression.

   a. $(-2)(-7x)$ **b.** $-(y)^2$

SOLUTION

   a. $(-2)(-7x) = 14x$ Two negative factors, so product is positive

   b. $-(y)^2 = (-1)(y^2) = -y^2$ One negative factor, so product is negative

Exercises for Example 2

Simplify the variable expression.

   7. $(5)(-w)$ **8.** $8(-t)(-t)$ **9.** $(-7)(-y)(-y)$

   10. $-\frac{1}{3}(6x)$ **11.** $-4(a)(-a)(-a)$ **12.** $-\frac{3}{5}(-s)(10s)$

EXAMPLE 3 *Evaluating a Variable Expression*

Evaluate the expression $(-12 \cdot x)(-3)$ when $x = -2$.

SOLUTION

$(-12 \cdot x)(-3) = 36x$ Simplify expression first.

$\qquad\qquad\qquad = 36(-2)$ Substitute -2 for x.

$\qquad\qquad\qquad = -72$ Simplify.

Exercises for Example 3

Evaluate the expression.

   13. $-15x$ when $x = 3$ **14.** $2p^2$ when $p = -1$

   15. $(-4m^2)(5m)$ when $m = -2$ **16.** k^3 when $k = -3$

Algebra 1, Concepts and Skills
Practice Workbook with Examples

NAME _____ DATE _____

Practice with Examples
For use with pages 92–98

EXAMPLE 4 *Using Multiplication in Real Life*

To promote its grand opening, a record store advertises compact discs for $10. The store loses $2.50 on each compact disc it sells. How much money will the store lose on its grand opening sale if it sells 256 discs?

SOLUTION

Multiply the number of discs sold by the loss per disc to find the total loss:

$$(256)(-2.50) = -640$$

The store loses $640 on its grand opening sale.

Exercises for Example 4

17. Rework Example 4 if the store loses $1.50 on each disc.

18. Rework Example 4 if the store sells 185 discs.

NAME _____ DATE _____

Practice with Examples

For use with pages 99–106

GOAL **Use the distributive property.**

> **VOCABULARY**
>
> **Distributive property:** the product of *a* and *b* + *c* or of *a* and *b* − *c*:
>
> $$a(b + c) = ab + ac \qquad a(b - c) = ab - ac$$
> $$(b + c)a = ba + ca \qquad (b - c)a = ba - ca$$

EXAMPLE 1 *Use an Area Model*

Find the area of a rectangle whose width is 5 and whose length is $x + 3$.

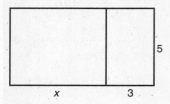

SOLUTION

Area = length × width

$= (x + 3)5$

$= 5x + 15$

Exercises for Example 1

1. Write two expressions for the area of the rectangle below.

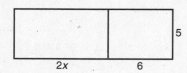

2. Write an algebraic statement that shows that the two expressions from Exercise 1 are equal.

Practice with Examples

For use with pages 99–106

EXAMPLE 2 *Use the Distributive Property with Addition*

Use the distributive property to rewrite the expression without parentheses.

   a. $-4(2x + 1)$ **b.** $(3x + 3)5$

SOLUTION

   a. $-8x - 4$ **b.** $15x + 15$

Exercises for Example 2

Use the distributive property to rewrite the expression without parentheses.

  3. $3(2x + 6)$ **4.** $-5(6x + 1)$ **5.** $-1(x + 8)$

EXAMPLE 3 *Use the Distributive Property with Subtraction*

Use the distributive property to rewrite the expression without parentheses.

   a. $4(x - 6)$ **b.** $-3(2x - 8)$

SOLUTION

   a. $4x - 24$ **b.** $-6x + 24$

Exercises for Example 3

Use the distributive property to rewrite the expression without parentheses.

  6. $-3(2x - 9)$ **7.** $(4x - 3)6$ **8.** $\frac{1}{2}(6x - 10)$

Practice with Examples

For use with pages 99–106

EXAMPLE 4 *Mental Math Calculations*

Use the distributive property to mentally calculate 23×6.

SOLUTION

$23 \times 6 = (20 + 3)6 = 20 \cdot 6 + 3 \cdot 6 = 120 + 18 = 138$

Exercises for Example 4

Use the distributive property to mentally calculate the expression.

9. 16×3 **10.** 2×38 **11.** 24×4

NAME _____ DATE _____

Practice with Examples

For use with pages 107–112

GOAL **Simplify an expression by combining like terms.**

VOCABULARY

The **coefficient** of a term is the number part of the product of a number and a variable.

Like terms are terms in an expression that have the same variable raised to the same power.

An expression is **simplified** if it has no grouping symbols and all the like terms have been combined.

EXAMPLE 1 *Identify Like Terms*

Identify the like terms in the expression $2x - 3x^2 + 4 - 5x - 3 + 2x^2$.

SOLUTION

The terms $-3x^2$ and $2x^2$ are like terms; the terms $2x$ and $-5x$ are like terms; and 4 and -3 are like terms.

Exercises for Example 1

Identify the like terms in the expression.

1. $5 - 2x + 3x^2 + 1 - 2x^2$ **2.** $6x + 10x^2 - 2x + 3 - 5x^2$

EXAMPLE 2 *Combine Like Terms*

Simplify the expression.

a. $5x^2 - 3x - 2x^2 + 4x$ **b.** $3 + 2x - 6x^2 - x + 1$

SOLUTION

a. $3x^2 + x$ **b.** $-6x^2 + x + 4$

Exercises for Example 2

Simplify the expression.

3. $4 - 6x + 2x^2 - 3 + 5x - 4x^2$ **4.** $3x^2 - 2 + 5x^2 - 8x - 3x^2 + 2$

Algebra 1, Concepts and Skills
Practice Workbook with Examples

NAME _____ DATE _____

Practice with Examples

For use with pages 107–112

EXAMPLE 3 *Simplify Expressions with Grouping Symbols*

a. $7 - 3(2 + z) = 7 + (-3)(2 + z)$ Rewrite as an addition expression.

$\qquad = 7 + [(-3)(2) + (-3)(z)]$ Distribute the -3.

$\qquad = 7 + (-6) + (-3z)$ Multiply.

$\qquad = 1 - 3z$ Combine like terms and simplify.

b. $4x(5 - x) - 2x = 4x[5 + (-x)] - 2x$ Rewrite as an addition expression.

$\qquad = (4x)(5) + (4x)(-x) - 2x$ Distribute the $4x$.

$\qquad = 20x - 4x^2 - 2x$ Multiply.

$\qquad = 20x - 2x - 4x^2$ Group like terms.

$\qquad = 18x - 4x^2$ Combine like terms and simplify.

Exercises for Example 3

Simplify the expression.

5. $(2w + 4)(-3) + w$ **6.** $3(5 - q) - q$ **7.** $-9t(t - 4) - 12$

8. $x^2 - 2x(x + 7)$ **9.** $-(6y - 5) + 6y$ **10.** $15d^2 + (2 - d)4d$

Algebra 1, Concepts and Skills
Practice Workbook with Examples

Practice with Examples

For use with pages 107–112

EXAMPLE 4 *Simplify a Function*

Every week on Saturday and Sunday you work a total of 8 hours doing lawn care and odd jobs for a neighbor. On Saturday you earn $10 per hour and on Sunday you earn $12 per hour.

 a. Write and simplify a function that gives the total amount you earn.

 b. If you work 5 hours on Saturday, how much do you earn?

SOLUTION

 a. Labels: Earnings $= e$
            Saturday hourly rate $= \$10$
            Hours worked Saturday $= t$
            Sunday hourly rate $= \$12$
            Hours worked Sunday $= 8 - t$

  $e = 10t + 12(8 - t)$

   $= 10t + 96 - 12t$

   $= -2t + 96$

 b. $e = -2t + 96$

   $= -2(5) + 96$

   $= 86$

 You earn $86.

Exercise for Example 4

11. A tailor is making draperies and 6 seat cushions to match for a dining room. The drapery material costs $25.00 per yard. The seat cushion material costs $20 per yard. The total amount of material needed is 21 yards. The tailor needs x yards for the drapes.

 a. Write and simplify a function that gives the total cost C of the materials.

 b. If the drapes use 12 yards of material, how much does all the material cost?

Algebra 1, Concepts and Skills
Practice Workbook with Examples

NAME _____ DATE _____

Practice with Examples

For use with pages 113–118

GOAL **Divide real numbers and use division to simplify algebraic expressions.**

> **VOCABULARY**
>
> Two numbers whose product is 1 are called **reciprocals**.

EXAMPLE 1 *Dividing Real Numbers*

Find the quotient.

a. $-30 \div 10$ **b.** $-24 \div (-6)$ **c.** $5 \div \left(-\frac{1}{3}\right)$

SOLUTION

a. $-30 \div 10 = -30 \cdot \frac{1}{10} = -3$

b. $-24 \div (-6) = -24 \cdot \left(-\frac{1}{6}\right) = 4$

c. $5 \div \left(-\frac{1}{3}\right) = 5(-3) = -15$

Exercises for Example 1

Find the quotient.

1. $36 \div (-3)$ **2.** $-28 \div (-7)$ **3.** $-13 \div 26$

4. $4 \div \left(-\frac{1}{2}\right)$ **5.** $-\frac{1}{3} \div (-5)$ **6.** $-25 \div 5$

EXAMPLE 2 *Simplifying Complex Fractions*

Find the quotient $\dfrac{-9}{\frac{3}{4}}$.

SOLUTION

$\dfrac{-9}{\frac{3}{4}} = -9 \div \dfrac{3}{4}$ Rewrite fraction as division expression.

$= -9\left(\dfrac{4}{3}\right)$ Multiply by reciprocal.

$= -12$ Simplify.

Practice with Examples

For use with pages 113–118

Exercises for Example 2

Simplify the expression.

7. $\dfrac{-12}{\frac{4}{3}}$

8. $\dfrac{24}{-\frac{1}{6}}$

9. $\dfrac{\frac{1}{2}}{-8}$

EXAMPLE 3 *Evaluating an Expression*

Evaluate the expression $\dfrac{3c + d}{d}$ when $c = -4$ and $d = -2$.

SOLUTION

$$\frac{3c + d}{d} = \frac{3(-4) + (-2)}{-2} = \frac{-12 + (-2)}{-2} = \frac{-14}{-2} = 7$$

Exercises for Example 3

Evaluate the expression for the given value(s) of the variable(s).

10. $\dfrac{2m - 9}{3}$ when $m = 6$

11. $\dfrac{y - 2x}{x}$ when $y = 8$ and $x = 2$

12. $\dfrac{11 - q}{7}$ when $q = -3$

13. $\dfrac{5a + 2b}{a}$ when $a = -1$ and $b = -2$

NAME _____   DATE _____

Practice with Examples

For use with pages 113–118

EXAMPLE 4 *Simplifying an Expression*

Simplify $\dfrac{12x - 9}{3}$.

SOLUTION

$$\dfrac{12x - 9}{3} = (12x - 9) \div 3 \qquad \text{Rewrite fraction as division expression.}$$

$$= (12x - 9) \cdot \dfrac{1}{3} \qquad \text{Multiply by reciprocal.}$$

$$= (12x)\left(\dfrac{1}{3}\right) - (9)\left(\dfrac{1}{3}\right) \qquad \text{Use distributive property.}$$

$$= 4x - 3 \qquad \text{Multiply.}$$

Exercises for Example 4

Simplify the expression.

14. $\dfrac{14t + 21}{7}$

15. $\dfrac{10x - 25}{-5}$

16. $\dfrac{-51y - 34}{17}$

Practice with Examples

For use with pages 131–137

GOAL Solve linear equations using addition and subtraction

VOCABULARY

Equivalent equations have the same solutions.

Inverse operations are two operations that undo each other, such as addition and subtraction.

Each time you apply a transformation to an equation, you are writing a **solution step.**

In a **linear equation,** the variable is raised to the *first* power and does not occur inside a square root symbol, an absolute value symbol, or in a denominator.

EXAMPLE 1 *Adding to Each Side*

Solve $y - 7 = -2$.

SOLUTION

To isolate y, you need to undo the subtraction by applying the inverse operation of adding 7.

$$y - 7 = -2 \qquad \text{Write original equation.}$$
$$y - 7 + 7 = -2 + 7 \qquad \text{Add 7 to each side.}$$
$$y = 5 \qquad \text{Simplify.}$$

The solution is 5. Check by substituting 5 for y in the original equation.

Exercises for Example 1

Solve the equation.

1. $t - 11 = 4$ **2.** $x - 2 = -3$ **3.** $5 = d - 8$

Practice with Examples

For use with pages 131–137

EXAMPLE 2 *Subtracting from Each Side*

Solve $q + 4 = -9$.

SOLUTION

To isolate q, you need to undo the addition by applying the inverse operation of subtracting 4.

$$q + 4 = -9 \qquad \text{Write original equation.}$$
$$q + 4 - 4 = -9 - 4 \qquad \text{Subtract 4 from each side.}$$
$$q = -13 \qquad \text{Simplify.}$$

The solution is -13. Check by substituting -13 for q in the original equation.

Exercises for Example 2
Solve the equation.

4. $s + 1 = -8$

5. $-6 + b = 10$

6. $6 = w + 12$

EXAMPLE 3 *Simplifying First*

Solve $x - (-3) = 10$.

SOLUTION

$$x - (-3) = 10 \qquad \text{Write original equation.}$$
$$x + 3 = 10 \qquad \text{Simplify.}$$
$$x + 3 - 3 = 10 - 3 \qquad \text{Subtract 3 from each side.}$$
$$x = 7 \qquad \text{Simplify.}$$

The solution is 7. Check by substituting 7 for x in the original equation.

Practice with Examples

For use with pages 131–137

Exercises for Example 3

Solve the equation.

7. $8 + z = 1$ **8.** $7 = k - 2$ **9.** $9 = a + (-5)$

EXAMPLE 4 *Modeling a Real-Life Problem*

The original price of a bicycle was marked down $20 to a sale price of $85. What was the original price?

SOLUTION

Original price (p) − Price reduction (20) = Sale Price (85)

Solve the equation $p - 20 = 85$.

$$p - 20 = 85 \qquad \text{Write real-life equation.}$$
$$p - 20 + 20 = 85 + 20 \qquad \text{Add 20 to each side.}$$
$$p = 105 \qquad \text{Simplify.}$$

The original price was $105. Check this in the statement of the problem.

Exercise for Example 4

10. After a sale, the price of a stereo was marked up $35 to a regular price of $310. What was the sale price?

Algebra 1, Concepts and Skills
Practice Workbook with Examples

Practice with Examples

For use with pages 138–143

GOAL **Solve linear equations using multiplication and division.**

> **VOCABULARY**
>
> **Properties of equality** are rules of algebra that can be used to transform equations into equivalent equations.

EXAMPLE 1 *Dividing Each Side of an Equation*

Solve $7n = -35$.

SOLUTION

To isolate n, you need to undo the multiplication by applying the inverse operation of dividing by 7.

$$7n = -35 \qquad \text{Write original equation.}$$

$$\frac{7n}{7} = \frac{-35}{7} \qquad \text{Divide each side by 7.}$$

$$n = -5 \qquad \text{Simplify.}$$

The solution is -5. Check by substituting -5 for n in the original equation.

Exercises for Example 1

Solve the equation.

1. $-12x = 6$

2. $4 = 24y$

3. $-5z = -35$

NAME _____ DATE _____

Practice with Examples

For use with pages 138–143

EXAMPLE 2 *Multiplying Each Side of an Equation*

Solve $-\dfrac{3}{4}t = 9$.

SOLUTION

To isolate t, you need to multiply by the reciprocal of the fraction.

$$-\frac{3}{4}t = 9 \qquad \text{Write original equation.}$$

$$\left(-\frac{4}{3}\right)\left(-\frac{3}{4}\right)t = \left(-\frac{4}{3}\right)9 \qquad \text{Multiply each side by } -\frac{4}{3}.$$

$$t = -12 \qquad \text{Simplify.}$$

The solution is -12. Check by substituting -12 for t in the original equation.

Exercises for Example 2

Solve the equation.

4. $\dfrac{1}{6}c = -2$
5. $\dfrac{f}{7} = 3$
6. $\dfrac{2}{3}q = 12$

Practice with Examples

For use with pages 138–143

EXAMPLE 3 *Modeling a Real-Life Problem*

Write and solve an equation to find your average speed s on a plane
flight. You flew 525 miles in 1.75 hours.

SOLUTION

**Verbal
Model** $\boxed{\text{Speed of jet}} \cdot \boxed{\text{Time}} = \boxed{\text{Distance}}$

Labels Speed of jet $= s$ (miles per hour)
Time $= 1.75$ (hours)
Distance $= 525$ (miles)

**Algebraic
Model** $s(1.75) = 525$ Write algebraic model.

$\dfrac{s(1.75)}{1.75} = \dfrac{525}{1.75}$ Divide each side by 1.75.

$s = 300$ Simplify.

The speed s was 300 miles per hour. Check this in the statement of the problem.

Exercises for Example 3

7. Write and solve an equation to find your
average speed in an airplane if you flew
800 miles in 2.5 hours.

8. Write and solve an equation to find
your time in an airplane if you flew
1530 miles at a speed of 340 miles
per hour.

Algebra 1, Concepts and Skills
Practice Workbook with Examples

NAME _____ DATE _____

Practice with Examples

For use with pages 144–149

GOAL Use two or more steps to solve a linear equation

EXAMPLE 1 *Solving a Linear Equation*

Solve $-3x - 4 = 5$.

SOLUTION

To isolate the variable x, undo the subtraction and then the multiplication.

$$-3x - 4 = 5 \qquad \text{Write original equation.}$$
$$-3x - 4 + 4 = 5 + 4 \qquad \text{Add 4 to each side.}$$
$$-3x = 9 \qquad \text{Simplify.}$$
$$\frac{-3x}{-3} = \frac{9}{-3} \qquad \text{Divide each side by } -3.$$
$$x = -3 \qquad \text{Simplify.}$$

The solution is -3. Check this in the original equation.

Exercises for Example 1

Solve the equation.

1. $5y + 8 = -2$

2. $7 - 6m = 1$

3. $\dfrac{x}{4} - 1 = 5$

Practice with Examples

For use with pages 144–149

EXAMPLE 2 *Using the Distributive Property and Combining Like Terms*

Solve $y + 5(y + 3) = 33$.

SOLUTION

$y + 5(y + 3) = 33$	Write original equation.
$y + 5y + 15 = 33$	Use distributive property.
$6y + 15 = 33$	Combine like terms.
$6y + 15 - 15 = 33 - 15$	Subtract 15 from each side.
$6y = 18$	Simplify.
$\dfrac{6y}{6} = \dfrac{18}{6}$	Divide each side by 6.
$y = 3$	Simplify.

The solution is 3. Check this in the original equation.

Exercises for Example 2

Solve the equation.

4. $4x - 8 + x = 2$ **5.** $6 - (b + 1) = 9$ **6.** $10(z - 2) = 1 + 4$

Practice with Examples

For use with pages 144–149

EXAMPLE 3 *Solving a Real-Life Problem*

The sum of the ages of two sisters is 25. The second sister's age is 5 more than three times the first sister's age n. Find the two ages.

SOLUTION

Verbal Model

First sister's age	$+$	Second sister's age	$=$	Sum

Labels
First sister's age = n (years)
Second sister's age = $3n + 5$ (years)
Sum = 25   (years)

Algebraic Model

$$n + (3n + 5) = 25$$ Write real-life equation.

$$4n + 5 = 25$$ Combine like terms.

$$4n + 5 - 5 = 25 - 5$$ Subtract 5 from each side.

$$4n = 20$$ Simplify.

$$\frac{4n}{4} = \frac{20}{4}$$ Divide each side by 4.

$$n = 5$$ Simplify.

The first sister's age is 5. The second sister's age is $3(5) + 5 = 20$.

Exercises for Example 3

7. A parking garage charges $3 plus $1.50 per hour. You have $12 to spend for parking. Write and solve an equation to find the number of hours that you can park.

8. As a lifeguard, you earn $6 per day plus $2.50 per hour. Write and solve an equation to find how many hours you must work to earn $16 in one day.

Algebra 1, Concepts and Skills
Practice Workbook with Examples

NAME _____ DATE _____

Practice with Examples

For use with pages 150–156

GOAL **Solve equations that have variables on both sides.**

> **VOCABULARY**
>
> An **identity** is an equation that is true for all values of the variable.

EXAMPLE 1 *Collecting Variables on One Side*

Solve $20 - 3x = 2x$.

SOLUTION

Think of $20 - 3x$ as $20 + (-3x)$. Since $2x$ is greater than $-3x$, collect the x-terms on the right side.

$$20 - 3x = 2x \qquad \text{Write original equation.}$$
$$20 - 3x + 3x = 2x + 3x \qquad \text{Add } 3x \text{ to each side.}$$
$$20 = 5x \qquad \text{Simplify.}$$
$$\frac{20}{5} = \frac{5x}{5} \qquad \text{Divide each side by 5.}$$
$$4 = x \qquad \text{Simplify.}$$

Exercises for Example 1

Solve the equation.

1. $5q = -7q + 6$ **2.** $14d - 6 = 17d$ **3.** $-y + 7 = -8y$

NAME _____ DATE _____

Practice with Examples

For use with pages 150–156

EXAMPLE 2 *Identifying the Number of Solutions*

a. Solve $2x + 3 = 2x + 4$. **b.** Solve $-(t + 5) = -t - 5$.

SOLUTION

a.
$2x + 3 = 2x + 4$	Write original equation.
$2x + 3 - 3 = 2x + 4 - 3$	Subtract 3 from each side.
$2x = 2x + 1$	Simplify.
$0 = 1$	Subtract $2x$ from each side.

The original equation has *no solution*, because $0 \neq 1$ for any value of x.

b.
$-(t + 5) = -t - 5$	Write original equation.
$-t - 5 = -t - 5$	Use distributive property.
$-5 = -5$	Add t to each side.

All values of t are solutions, because $-5 = -5$ is always true.
The original equation is an *identity*.

Exercises for Example 2

Solve the equation.

4. $9z - 3 = 9z$ **5.** $2(f - 7) = 2f - 14$ **6.** $n + 3 = -5n$

Practice with Examples

For use with pages 150–156

EXAMPLE 3 *Solving Real-Life Problems*

A health club charges nonmembers $2 per day to swim and $5 per day for aerobics classes. Members pay a yearly fee of $200 plus $3 per day for aerobics classes. Write and solve an equation to find the number of days you must use the club to justify a yearly membership.

SOLUTION

Let n represent the number of days that you use the club. Then find the number of times for which the two plans would cost the same.

$2n + 5n = 200 + 3n$	Write equation.
$7n = 200 + 3n$	Combine like terms.
$7n - 3n = 200 + 3n - 3n$	Subtract $3n$ from each side.
$4n = 200$	Simplify.
$\dfrac{4n}{4} = \dfrac{200}{4}$	Divide each side by 4.
$n = 50$	Simplify.

You must use the club 50 days to justify a yearly membership.

Exercises for Example 3

7. Rework Example 3 if nonmembers pay $3 per day to swim.

8. Rework Example 3 if members pay a yearly fee of $220.

Algebra 1, Concepts and Skills
Practice Workbook with Examples

Practice with Examples

For use with pages 157–162

GOAL Solve more complicated equations that have variables on both sides.

EXAMPLE 1 *Solving a More Complicated Equation*

Solve the equation.

a. $2(x - 5) + 10 = -(-3x + 2)$

b. $-3(5x + 1) + 2x = 2(4x - 3)$

c. $\frac{1}{2}(16 - 6x) = 15 - \frac{1}{3}(9 + 15x)$

SOLUTION

a.
$2(x - 5) + 10 = -(-3x + 2)$	Write original equation.
$2x - 10 + 10 = 3x - 2$	Use distributive property.
$2x = 3x - 2$	Combine like terms.
$-x = -2$	Subtract $3x$ from each side.
$x = 2$	Divide each side by -1.

The solution is 2. Check this in the original equation.

b.
$-3(5x + 1) + 2x = 2(4x - 3)$	Write original equation.
$-15x - 3 + 2x = 8x - 6$	Use distributive property.
$-13x - 3 = 8x - 6$	Combine like terms.
$-21x - 3 = -6$	Subtract $8x$ from each side.
$-21x = -3$	Add 3 to each side.
$x = \frac{1}{7}$	Divide each side by -21.

The solution is $\frac{1}{7}$. Check this in the original equation.

LESSON

3.5

CONTINUED

NAME _____ DATE _____

Practice with Examples

For use with pages 157–162

c. $\frac{1}{2}(16 - 6x) = 15 - \frac{1}{3}(9 + 15x)$ Write original equation.

$8 - 3x = 15 - 3 - 5x$ Use distributive property.

$8 - 3x = 12 - 5x$ Combine like terms.

$8 + 2x = 12$ Add $5x$ to each side.

$2x = 4$ Subtract 8 from each side.

$x = 2$ Divide each side by 2.

The solution is 2. Check this in the original equation.

Exercises for Example 1

1. $2(x + 5) + 3x = 3(-2x - 1)$ **2.** $\frac{3}{4}(8x - 20) = 6x + 12 - 12x$

EXAMPLE 2   *Drawing a Diagram*

The front page of your school newspaper is $11\frac{1}{4}$ inches wide. The left margin is 1 inch and the right margin is $1\frac{1}{2}$ inches. The space between the four columns is $\frac{1}{4}$ inch. Find the width of each column.

SOLUTION

The diagram shows that the page is made up of the width of the left margin, the width of the right margin, three spaces between the columns, and the four columns.

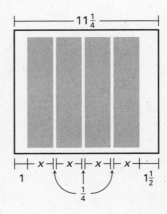

Algebra 1, Concepts and Skills
Practice Workbook with Examples

Practice with Examples

For use with pages 157–162

| **Verbal Model** | Left margin | + | Right margin | + 3 · | Space between columns | + 4 · | Column width | = | Page width |

Labels   Left margin = 1   (inch)

Right margin = $1\frac{1}{2}$ (inches)

Space between columns = $\frac{1}{4}$ (inch)

Column width = x (inches)

Page width = $11\frac{1}{4}$ (inches)

Algebraic Model $1 + 1\frac{1}{2} + 3\left(\frac{1}{4}\right) + 4x = 11\frac{1}{4}$

Solving for x, you find that each column can be 2 inches wide.

Exercise for Example 2

3. Rework Example 2 if the front page of the newspaper has three columns.

Practice with Examples

For use with pages 163–170

GOAL Find exact and approximate solutions of equations that contain decimals.

VOCABULARY

A **rounding error** occurs when you use solutions that are not exact.

EXAMPLE 1 *Rounding for the Final Answer*

Solve $412x - 1640 = 238x - 12$. Round the result to the nearest hundredth.

SOLUTION

$412x - 1640 = 238x - 12$	Write original equation.
$174x - 1640 = -12$	Subtract $238x$ from each side.
$174x = 1628$	Add 1640 to each side.
$x = \dfrac{1628}{174}$	Divide each side by 174.
$x \approx 9.35632$	Use a calculator.
$x \approx 9.36$	Round to the nearest hundredth.

The solution is approximately 9.36.

Exercises for Example 1

Solve the equation. Round the result to the nearest hundredth.

1. $21x + 60 = 72$

2. $23 - 5x = 114x + 30$

3. $44y - 18 = y + 17$

4. $12b - 93 = 54b - 142$

Practice with Examples

For use with pages 163–170

EXAMPLE 2 *Solving an Equation Containing Decimals*

Solve $3.11x - 11.75 = 2.02x$. Round to the nearest hundredth.

SOLUTION

$3.11x - 11.75 = 2.02x$	Write original equation.
$1.09x - 11.75 = 0$	Subtract $2.02x$ from each side.
$1.09x = 11.75$	Add 11.75 to each side.
$x = \frac{11.75}{1.09}$	Divide each side by 1.09.
$x \approx 10.77981$	Use a calculator.
$x \approx 10.78$	Round to nearest hundredth.

The solution is approximately 10.78. Check this in the original equation.

Exercises for Example 2

Solve the equation and round to the nearest hundredth.

5. $22.5 + 3.2x = 3.4x$

6. $-0.83y + 0.17 = 0.72y$

Practice with Examples

For use with pages 163–170

EXAMPLE 3 *Using a Verbal Model*

While dining at a restaurant, you want to leave a 15% tip. You have a total of $14.00 to spend. What is your price limit for the dinner? Using the verbal model below, write and solve an algebraic equation.

$$\boxed{\text{Price limit}} \ + \ \boxed{\text{Tip rate}} \ \cdot \ \boxed{\text{Price limit}} \ = \ \boxed{\text{Total cost}}$$

SOLUTION

Let x represent your price limit.

$x + 0.15x = 14.00$	Write algebraic model.
$1.15x = 14.00$	Combine like terms.
$x = \dfrac{14.00}{1.15}$	Divide each side by 1.15.
$x \approx 12.173913$	Use a calculator.
$x \approx 12.17$	Round down.

The answer is rounded *down* to $12.17 because you have a limited amount to spend.

Exercises for Example 3

7. Rework Example 3 if you have $16.00 to spend.

8. Rework Example 3 if you want to leave a 20% tip.

Practice with Examples

For use with pages 171–176

GOAL **Solve a formula for one of its variables**

> **VOCABULARY**
>
> A **formula** is an algebraic equation that relates two or more real-life quantities.

EXAMPLE 1 *Solving and Using an Area Formula*

Use the formula for the area of a rectangle, $A = \ell w$.

a. Solve the formula for the width w.

b. Use the new formula to find the width of a rectangle that has an area of 72 square inches and a length of 9 inches.

SOLUTION

a. Solve for width w.

$$A = \ell w \qquad \text{Write original formula.}$$

$$\frac{A}{\ell} = \frac{\ell w}{\ell} \qquad \text{To isolate } w, \text{ divide each side by } \ell.$$

$$\frac{A}{\ell} = w \qquad \text{Simplify.}$$

b. Substitute the given values into the new formula.

$$w = \frac{A}{\ell} = \frac{72}{9} = 8$$

The width of the rectangle is 8 inches.

Exercises for Example 1

Solve for the indicated variable.

1. Area of a Triangle

Solve for h: $A = \frac{1}{2}bh$

2. Circumference of a Circle

Solve for r: $C = 2\pi r$

3. Simple Interest
Solve for P: $I = Prt$

4. Simple Interest
Solve for r: $I = Prt$

Practice with Examples

For use with pages 171–176

EXAMPLE 2 *Solving and Using a Distance Formula*

Driving on the highway, you travel 930 miles at an average speed of 62 miles per hour.

a. Solve the distance formula $d = rt$ for time t.

b. Estimate the time spent driving.

SOLUTION

a. $d = rt$ Write original formula.

$\dfrac{d}{r} = t$ Divide each side by r.

b. Substitute the given values for the new formula.

$t = \dfrac{d}{r}$ Write formula.

$t = \dfrac{930}{62}$ Substitute 930 for d and 62 for r.

$t = 1.5$ Solve for t.

Answer You spent approximately 1.5 hours driving.

Practice with Examples

For use with pages 171–176

Exercises for Example 2

5. Solve the distance formula for *r*.

6. Use the result from Exercise 5 to find the average speed in miles per hour of a car that travels 1275 miles in 22 hours. Round your answer to the nearest whole number.

NAME _____ DATE _____

Practice with Examples

For use with pages 177–182

GOAL   **Use ratios and rates to solve real-life problems.**

VOCABULARY

If a and b are two quantities measured in different units, then the **rate of a per b** is $\dfrac{a}{b}$.

A **unit rate** is a rate per one given unit.

EXAMPLE 1   *Finding a Ratio*

The team won 12 of its 15 games. Find the ratio of wins to losses.

SOLUTION

$$\text{Ratio} = \frac{\text{games won}}{\text{games lost}} = \frac{12 \text{ games}}{3 \text{ games}} = \frac{4}{1}$$

Exercise for Example 1

1. You answer correctly 48 of the 50 questions on a quiz. Find the ratio of correct answers to incorrect answers.

EXAMPLE 2   *Finding a Unit Rate*

You hike 24 miles in 2 days. What is your average speed in miles per day?

SOLUTION

$$\text{Ratio} = \frac{24 \text{ miles}}{2 \text{ days}} = \frac{12 \text{ miles}}{1 \text{ day}} = 12 \text{ mi/day}$$

NAME _____ DATE _____

Practice with Examples

For use with pages 177–182

Exercises for Example 2

Find the unit rate.

2. A car drives 120 miles in 3 hours.

3. You earn $55 for working 5 hours.

EXAMPLE 3 *Using a Rate*

You took a survey of your classmates and found that 9 of the 27 class-mates have public library cards. Use your results to make a prediction for the 855 students enrolled in your school.

SOLUTION

You can answer the question by writing a ratio. Let n represent the number of students in your school that have public library cards.

$$\frac{\text{Library cards in sample}}{\text{Total students in sample}} = \frac{\text{Library cards in school}}{\text{Total students in school}}$$

$$\frac{9}{27} = \frac{n}{855} \qquad \text{Write equation.}$$

$$855 \cdot \frac{9}{27} = n \qquad \text{Multiply each side by 855.}$$

$$285 = n \qquad \text{Simplify.}$$

Of the 855 students enrolled in the school, about 285 will have a public library card.

Exercises for Example 3

4. Rework Example 3 if 6 of the 27 class-mates have public library cards.

5. Rework Example 3 if 930 students are enrolled in the school.

Practice with Examples

For use with pages 177–182

EXAMPLE 4 *Applying Unit Analysis*

While visiting Italy you want to exchange $120 for liras. The rate of currency exchange is 1850 liras per United States dollar. How many liras will you receive?

SOLUTION

You can use unit analysis to write an equation.

$$\text{dollars} \cdot \frac{\text{liras}}{\text{dollars}} = \text{liras}$$

$$D \cdot \frac{1850}{1} = L \qquad \text{Write equation.}$$

$$120 \cdot \frac{1850}{1} = L \qquad \text{Substitute 120 for } D \text{ dollars.}$$

$$222{,}000 = L \qquad \text{Simplify.}$$

You will receive 222,000 liras.

Exercises for Example 4

Convert the currency using the given exchange rate.

6. Convert $150 U.S. dollars to German marks. ($1 U.S. is 1.8943 marks)

7. Convert $200 U.S. dollars to Austrian schillings. ($1 U.S. is 13.3272 schillings)

Algebra 1, Concepts and Skills
Practice Workbook with Examples

NAME _____ DATE _____

Practice with Examples

For use with pages 183–188

GOAL Solve percent problems.

VOCABULARY

A **percent** is a ratio that compares a number to 100.
In any percent equation the **base number** is the number that you are comparing to.

EXAMPLE 1 *Number Compared to Base is Unknown*

What is 40% of 65 meters?

SOLUTION

Verbal Model $\boxed{a}$ is $\boxed{p\ \text{percent}}$ of $\boxed{b}$

Labels   Number compared to base $= a$ (meters)

   Percent $= 40\% = 0.40$ (no units)

   Base number $= 65$ (meters)

Algebraic Model $a = (0.40)(65)$

   $a = 26$ 26 meters is 40% of 65 meters.

Exercises for Example 1

1. What is 24% of $30?

2. What is 60% of 15 miles?

Algebra 1, Concepts and Skills
Practice Workbook with Examples

NAME _____ DATE _____

Practice with Examples

For use with pages 183–188

EXAMPLE 2 *Base Number is Unknown*

Twenty-five miles is 20% of what distance?

SOLUTION

Verbal Model	$\boxed{a}$ is $\boxed{p \text{ percent}}$ of $\boxed{b}$
Labels	Number compared to base = 25 (miles)
	Percent = 20% = 0.20 (no units)
	Base number = b (miles)
Algebraic Model	$25 = (0.20)b$
	$\dfrac{25}{0.20} = 125 = b$ 25 miles is 20% of 125 miles.

Exercises for Example 2

3. Sixty grams is 40% of what weight?   **4.** Fifteen yards is 30% of what distance?

EXAMPLE 3 *Percent is Unknown*

Ninety is what percent of 15?

SOLUTION

Verbal Model	$\boxed{a}$ is $\boxed{p \text{ percent}}$ of $\boxed{b}$
Labels	Number compared to base = 90 (no units)
	Percent = $p\%$ = $\dfrac{p}{100}$ (no units)
	Base Number = 15 (no units)
Algebraic Model	$90 = \dfrac{p}{100}(15)$
	$\dfrac{90}{15} = \dfrac{p}{100}$
	$6 = p$
	$600\% = p$
	90 is 600% of 15.

NAME _____ DATE _____

Practice with Examples
For use with pages 183–188

Exercises for Example 3

5. Forty-five is what percent of 180?

6. Sixty is what percent of 15?

EXAMPLE 4 **Modeling and Using Percents**

You took a multiple-choice exam with 200 questions. You answered 80% of the questions correctly. How many questions did you answer correctly?

SOLUTION

You can solve the problem by using a proportion. Let n represent the number of correct answers.

$$\frac{Number\ of\ correct\ answers}{Total\ number\ of\ answers} = \frac{80}{100} \qquad \text{Write proportion.}$$

$$\frac{n}{200} = \frac{80}{100} \qquad \text{Substitute.}$$

$$100n = 200 \cdot 80 \qquad \text{Use cross products.}$$

$$n = \frac{200 \cdot 80}{100} \qquad \text{Divide by 100.}$$

$$n = 160 \qquad \text{Simplify.}$$

You answered 160 questions correctly.

Exercise for Example 4

7. Rework Example 4 if you answered 85% of the questions correctly.

Algebra 1, Concepts and Skills
Practice Workbook with Examples

NAME _____ DATE _____

Practice with Examples

For use with pages 203–208

GOAL Plot points in a coordinate plane.

VOCABULARY

A **coordinate plane**, which is divided into four regions called quadrants, is formed by two real number lines that intersect at a right angle. The point of intersection is the **origin**. The horizontal line is the **x-axis** and the vertical line is the **y-axis**.

Each point in a coordinate plane corresponds to an **ordered pair** of real numbers. The first number is the **x-coordinate** and the second number is the **y-coordinate.**

A **scatter plot** is a coordinate graph containing points that represent real-life data.

EXAMPLE 1 *Plotting Points in a Coordinate Plane*

Plot and label the following ordered pairs in a coordinate plane.

a. $(3, -2)$ **b.** $(-4, 3)$

SOLUTION

To plot a point, you move along the horizontal and vertical lines in the coordinate plane and mark the location that corresponds to the ordered pair.

a. To plot the point $(3, -2)$, start at the origin. Move 3 units to the right and 2 units down.

b. To plot the point $(-4, 3)$, start at the origin. Move 4 units to the left and 3 units up.

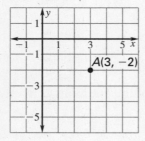
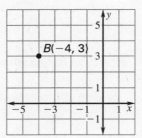

Exercises for Example 1

Plot and label the ordered pairs in a coordinate plane.

1. $A(5, 4), B(-3, 0), C(-1, -2)$ **2.** $A(-3, 2), B(0, 0), C(2, -2)$

NAME _____ DATE _____

Practice with Examples

For use with pages 203–208

Plot and label the ordered pairs in a coordinate plane.

3. $A(0, -4), B(3, 5), C(3, -1)$

4. $A(-1, -2), B(5, -2), C(-4, 0)$

5. $A(-1, 3), B(2, 0), C(3, -2)$

6. $A(2, 4), B(-2, 5), C(0, 3)$

EXAMPLE 2 *Sketching a Scatter Plot*

The table below gives the U.S. postal rates (in cents) for first-class mail, based on the weight (in ounces) of the mail. Draw a scatter plot of the data and predict the postal rate for a piece of mail that weighs 8 ounces.

Weight (ounces)	1	2	3	4	5
Rate (cents)	33	55	77	99	121

SOLUTION

❶ Rewrite the data in the table as a list of ordered pairs.

   (1, 33), (2, 55), (3, 77), (4, 99), (5, 121)

❷ Draw a coordinate plane. Put weight w on the horizontal axis and rate r on the vertical axis.

❸ Plot the points.

❹ From the scatter plot, you can see that the points follow a pattern. By extending the pattern, you can predict that the postal rate for an 8 ounce piece of mail is about 187 cents, or $1.87.

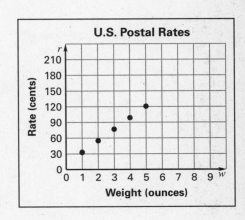

NAME _____ DATE _____

Practice with Examples

For use with pages 203–208

Exercises for Example 2

In Exercises 7 and 8, make a scatter plot of the data. Use the horizontal axis to represent time.

7.

Year	1997	1998	1999	2000
Members	74	81	89	95

8.

Month	Jan.	Apr.	Aug.	Dec.
Adults	22	30	15	42

In Exercises 9 and 10, make a scatter plot of the data. Use the horizontal axis to represent quarts in Exercise 9 and hours in Exercise 10.

9.

Quarts	3.0	4.0	5.0	6.0
Gallons	0.75	1.0	1.25	1.5

10.

Hours	3	5	6	8
Rental charge (dollars)	12	20	24	32

Algebra 1, Concepts and Skills
Practice Workbook with Examples

Practice with Examples

For use with pages 209–215

GOAL Graph a linear equation using a table of values.

VOCABULARY

A linear equation in x and y is an equation that can be written in the form $Ax + By = C$, where A and B are not both zero.

A **solution of an equation** in two variables x and y is an ordered pair (x, y) that makes the equation true.

A two-variable equation is written in **function form** if one of the variables is isolated on one side of the equation.

The **graph of an equation** in x and y is the set of all points (x, y) that are solutions of the equation.

EXAMPLE 1 *Checking Solutions of Linear Equations*

Decide whether the point $(10, 1)$ is a solution of $x - 2y = 8$.

SOLUTION

$$x - 2y = 8 \qquad \text{Write original equation.}$$
$$10 - 2(1) \overset{?}{=} 8 \qquad \text{Substitute 10 for } x \text{ and 1 for } y.$$
$$8 = 8 \qquad \text{Simplify. True statement}$$

$(10, 1)$ is a solution of the equation $x - 2y = 8$.

Exercises for Example 1

Decide whether the given ordered pair is a solution of the equation.

1. $-3x + 6y = 12, (-4, 0)$

2. $x + 5y = 11, (2, 1)$

3. $y = 1, (3, 1)$

4. $3y - 5x = 4, (-2, 2)$

Practice with Examples

For use with pages 209–215

EXAMPLE 2 *Finding Solutions of Linear Equations*

Find three ordered pairs that are solutions to $3x + y = 1$.

SOLUTION

$$3x + y = 1$$
$$y = -3x + 1$$

x	-2	-1	0	1	2
y	7	4	1	-2	-5

$(-2, 7), (-1, 4)$ and $(0, 1)$ are three solutions of $3x + y = 1$.

Exercises for Example 2

Find three ordered pairs that are solutions of the equation.

5. $2x - y = 8$ **6.** $3x + y = -2$

7. $y + 3 = 2x$ **8.** $y - 5 = 3x$

9. $3x + 4 = y$ **10.** $4x - 1 = y$

Algebra 1, Concepts and Skills
Practice Workbook with Examples

NAME _____ DATE _____

Practice with Examples

For use with pages 209–215

EXAMPLE 3 *Graphing a Linear Equation*

Use a table of values to graph the equation $x - 2y = 4$.

SOLUTION

Rewrite the equation in function form by solving for y.

$x - 2y = 4$	Write original equation.
$-2y = -x + 4$	Subtract x from each side.
$y = \dfrac{x}{2} - 2$	Divide each side by -2.

Choose a variety of values of x and make a table of values.

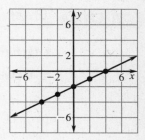

Choose x.	-4	-2	0	2	4
Evaluate y.	-4	-3	-2	-1	0

Using the table of values, you can write five ordered pairs.

$(-4, -4), (-2, -3), (0, -2), (2, -1), (4, 0)$

Plot each ordered pair. The line through the points is the graph of the equation.

Exercises for Example 3

Use a table of values to graph the equation.

11. $y = 3x - 4$

12. $3y - 3x = 6$

13. $y = -3(x - 1)$

Algebra 1, Concepts and Skills
Practice Workbook with Examples

Practice with Examples

For use with pages 216–221

GOAL **Graph horizontal and vertical lines.**

VOCABULARY

The graph of a linear equation of the form $By = C$, where $B \neq 0$, is a **horizontal line**.

The graph of a linear equation of the form $Ax = C$, where $A \neq 0$, is a **vertical line**.

A function of the form $y = b$, where b is a number, is called a **constant function**.

EXAMPLE 1 *Graphing y = b*

Graph the equation $y = -3$.

SOLUTION

The y-value is always -3, regardless of the value of x. The points $(-1, -3)$, $(0, -3)$, $(2, -3)$ are some solutions of the equation. The graph of the equation is a horizontal line 3 units below the x-axis.

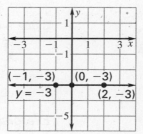

EXAMPLE 2 *Graphing x = a*

Graph the equation $x = 5$.

SOLUTION

The x-value is always 5, regardless of the value of y. The points $(5, -2)$, $(5, 0)$, $(5, 3)$ are some solutions of the equation. The graph of the equation is a vertical line 5 units to the right of the y-axis.

NAME _____ DATE _____

Practice with Examples

For use with pages 216–221

Exercises for Examples 1 and 2

Graph the equation.

1. $y = 0$ **2.** $x = -4$ **3.** $x = 0$

4. $y = 6$ **5.** $y = -5$ **6.** $x = 2$

EXAMPLE 3 *Write an Equation of a Line*

Write the equation of the line in the graph.

a.
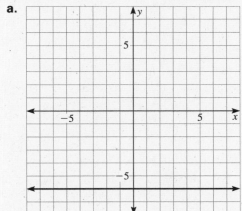

b.
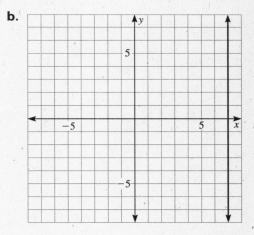

SOLUTION

a. The graph is a horizontal line 6 units below the x-axis. The y-coordinate is always -6.

   Answer ▶ $y = -6$

b. The graph is a vertical line 7 units to the right of the y-axis. The x-coordinate is always 7.

   Answer ▶ $x = 7$

Algebra 1, Concepts and Skills
Practice Workbook with Examples

NAME _____ DATE _____

Practice with Examples

For use with pages 216–221

Exercises for Example 3

Write the equation of the line in the graph.

7.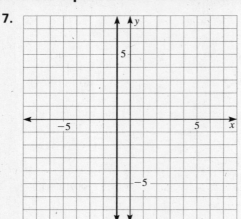

8.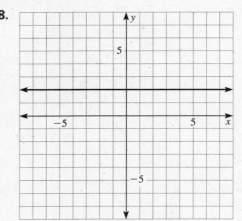

Algebra 1, Concepts and Skills
Practice Workbook with Examples

Practice with Examples

For use with pages 222–227

GOAL **Find the intercepts of the graph of a linear equation and then use them to make a quick graph of the equation.**

VOCABULARY

An **x-intercept** is the x-coordinate of a point where a graph crosses the x-axis. The y-coordinate of this point is 0.

A **y-intercept** is the y-coordinate of a point where a graph crosses the y-axis. The x-coordinate of this point is 0.

EXAMPLE 1 *Finding Intercepts*

_____

Find the x-intercept and the y-intercept of the graph of the equation $4x - 2y = 8$.

SOLUTION

To find the x-intercept of $4x - 2y = 8$, let $y = 0$.

$$4x - 2y = 8 \qquad \text{Write original equation.}$$
$$4x - 2(0) = 8 \qquad \text{Substitute 0 for } y.$$
$$x = 2 \qquad \text{Solve for } x.$$

The x-intercept is 2. The line crosses the x-axis at the point $(2, 0)$.

To find the y-intercept of $4x - 2y = 8$, let $x = 0$.

$$4x - 2y = 8 \qquad \text{Write original equation.}$$
$$4(0) - 2y = 8 \qquad \text{Substitute 0 for } x.$$
$$y = -4 \qquad \text{Solve for } y.$$

The y-intercept is -4. The line crosses the y-axis at the point $(0, -4)$.

Practice with Examples

For use with pages 222–227

Exercises for Example 1

Find the *x*-intercept of the graph of the equation.

1. $x - y = 6$

2. $-2x + y = -4$

3. $3x - 2y = 6$

Find the *y*-intercept of the graph of the equation.

4. $x - y = 6$

5. $-2x + y = -4$

6. $3x - 2y = 6$

EXAMPLE 2 *Making a Quick Graph*

Graph the equation $2x - y = 8$.

SOLUTION

Find the intercepts by first substituting 0 for *y* and then substituting 0 for *x*.

$$2x - y = 8 \qquad\qquad 2x - y = 8$$
$$2x - 0 = 8 \qquad\qquad 2(0) - y = 8$$
$$2x = 8 \qquad\qquad -y = 8$$
$$x = 4 \qquad\qquad y = -8$$

The *x*-intercept is 4.   The *y*-intercept is -8.

Draw a coordinate plane that includes the points $(4, 0)$ and $(0, -8)$. Plot the points $(4, 0)$ and $(0, -8)$ and draw a line through them. The graph is shown below.

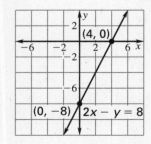

NAME _____ DATE _____

Practice with Examples

For use with pages 222–227

Exercises for Example 2

Find the *x*-intercept and the *y*-intercept of the line. Use the intercepts to sketch a quick graph of the equation.

7. $y = -x + 6$

8. $x - 5y = 15$

9. $y = 4 - 2x$

10. $7x - y = 14$

11. $3x + 4y = 24$

12. $2y = 7x + 10$

Algebra 1, Concepts and Skills
Practice Workbook with Examples

Practice with Examples

For use with pages 228–235

GOAL **Find the slope of a line.**

VOCABULARY

The **slope** m of a line is the ratio of the vertical **rise** to the horizontal **run** between any two points on the line.

The slope of a line that passes through the points (x_1, y_1) and (x_2, y_2) is given by $m = \dfrac{\text{rise}}{\text{run}} = \dfrac{\text{change in } y}{\text{change in } x} = \dfrac{y_2 - y_1}{x_2 - x_1}$.

EXAMPLE 1 *Finding the Slope of a Line*

Find the slope of the line passing through $(-3, 2)$ and $(1, 5)$.

SOLUTION

Let $(x_1, y_1) = (-3, 2)$ and $(x_2, y_2) = (1, 5)$.

$m = \dfrac{y_2 - y_1}{x_2 - x_1}$ ← Rise: Difference of y-values
                ← Run: Difference of x-values

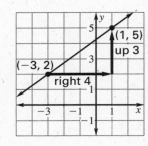

$= \dfrac{5 - 2}{1 - (-3)}$ Substitute values.

$= \dfrac{3}{1 + 3} = \dfrac{3}{4}$ Simplify. Slope is positive.

....

Because the slope in Example 1 is positive, the line rises from left to right. If a line has negative slope, then the line falls from left to right.

Practice with Examples

For use with pages 228–235

Exercises for Example 1

Plot the points and find the slope of the line passing through them.

1. $(-4, 0), (3, 3)$

2. $(-1, -2), (2, -6)$

3. $(-3, -1), (1, 3)$

Find the slope of the line that passes through the points.

4. $(5, 4), (3, 1)$

5. $(-2, 3), (0, 2)$

6. $(2, 4), (-1, -1)$

EXAMPLE 2 *Finding the Slope of a Line*

Find the slope of the line passing through $(-4, 2)$ and $(1, 2)$.

SOLUTION

Let $(x_1, y_1) = (-4, 2)$ and $(x_2, y_2) = (1, 2)$.

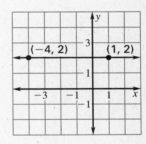

$$m = \frac{y_2 - y_1}{x_2 - x_1} \quad \leftarrow \text{ Rise: Difference of } y\text{-values}$$
$$\phantom{m = \frac{y_2 - y_1}{x_2 - x_1}} \quad \leftarrow \text{ Run: Difference of } x\text{-values}$$

$$= \frac{2 - 2}{1 - (-4)} \qquad \text{Substitute values.}$$

$$= \frac{0}{5} = 0 \qquad \text{Simplify. Slope is zero.}$$

Because the slope in Example 2 is zero, the line is horizontal. If the slope of a line is undefined, the line is vertical.

NAME _____ DATE _____

Practice with Examples

For use with pages 228–235

Exercises for Example 2

Plot the points and find the slope of the line passing through the points.

7. $(-4, 0), (-4, 3)$

8. $(1, -1), (1, 3)$

9. $(-3, 0), (1, 0)$

10. $(-4, 3), (1, 3)$

11. $(2, -2), (2, -6)$

12. $(-1, -6), (2, -6)$

Algebra 1, Concepts and Skills
Practice Workbook with Examples

Practice with Examples

For use with pages 236–241

GOAL **Write and graph equations that represent direct variation.**

VOCABULARY

Two quantities x and y that have a constant ratio k are said to have **direct variation.**

In the model for direct variation $y = kx$, the constant k is the **constant of variation.**

EXAMPLE 1 *Writing a Direct Variation Equation*

The variables x and y vary directly. When $x = 4$, $y = 6$.

a. Write an equation that relates x and y.

b. Find the value of y when $x = 12$.

SOLUTION

a. Because x and y vary directly, the equation is of the form $y = kx$. You can solve for k as follows.

$$y = kx \qquad \text{Write model for direct variation.}$$
$$6 = k(4) \qquad \text{Substitute 4 for } x \text{ and 6 for } y.$$
$$1.5 = k \qquad \text{Divide each side by 4.}$$

An equation that relates x and y is $y = 1.5x$.

b. $y = 1.5(12) \qquad \text{Substitute 12 for } x \text{ in } y = 1.5x.$
$y = 18 \qquad \text{Simplify.}$

When $x = 12$, $y = 18$.

Exercises for Example 1

The variables x and y vary directly. Use the given values to write an equation that relates x and y.

1. $x = 3, y = 15$ **2.** $x = 6, y = 3$

Algebra 1, Concepts and Skills
Practice Workbook with Examples

NAME _____ DATE _____

Practice with Examples

The variables *x* and *y* vary directly. Use the given values to write an equation that relates *x* and *y*.

3. $x = -4, y = -4$

4. $x = 10, y = -2$

5. $x = 3.5, y = 7$

6. $x = -12, y = 4$

EXAMPLE 2 *Using a Direct Variation Model*

Weight varies directly with gravity. A person who weighs 150 pounds on Earth weighs 57 pounds on Mars.

a. Write a model that relates a person's weight *E* on Earth to that person's weight *M* on Mars.

b. A person weighs 210 pounds on Earth. Use the model to estimate that person's weight on Mars.

SOLUTION

a. Because *M* and *E* vary directly, the equation is of the form $E = kM$.

$E = kM$ Write model for direct variation.

$150 = k(57)$ Substitute 57 for *M* and 150 for *E*.

$\dfrac{150}{7} = k$ Divide each side by 57.

The model for direct variation is $E = \dfrac{150}{57}M$.

b. Use the model $E = \dfrac{150}{57}M$ to estimate the person's weight on Mars.

$210 = \dfrac{150}{57}M$ Substitute 210 for *E*.

$79.8 \approx M$ Multiply each side by $\dfrac{57}{150}$.

The person weighs about 79.8 pounds on Mars.

NAME _____ DATE _____

Practice with Examples

For use with pages 236–241

Exercises for Example 2

7. Use the model $E = \frac{150}{57}M$ to estimate a person's weight on Mars if the person weighs 120 pounds on Earth.

8. Use the model $E = \frac{150}{57}M$ to estimate a person's weight on Earth if the person weighs 62 pounds on Mars.

9. A person who weighs 160 pounds on Earth weighs 139 pounds on Venus.
   a. Write a model that relates a person's weight E on Earth to that person's weight V on Venus.

   b. A person weighs 195 pounds on Earth. Use the model to estimate that person's weight on Venus.

Practice with Examples

For use with pages 242–251

GOAL Graph a linear equation in slope-intercept form.

VOCABULARY

The linear equation $y = mx + b$ is written in **slope-intercept form.** The slope of the line is m. The y-intercept is b.

Two different lines in the same plane are **parallel** if they do not intersect. Any two nonvertical lines are parallel if and only if they have the same slope and different y-intercepts. (All vertical lines are parallel.)

EXAMPLE 1 *Finding the Slope and y-Intercept*

EQUATION	SLOPE-INTERCEPT FORM	SLOPE	y-INTERCEPT
a. $y = 3x$	$y = 3x + 0$	$m = 3$	$b = 0$
b. $y = -\dfrac{3}{5} + \dfrac{2}{5}x$	$y = \dfrac{2}{5}x - \dfrac{3}{5}$	$m = \dfrac{2}{5}$	$b = -\dfrac{3}{5}$
c. $4x + 8y = 24$	$y = -0.5x + 3$	$m = -0.5$	$b = 3$

Exercises for Example 1

Write the equation in slope-intercept form. Find the slope and the y-intercept

1. $y = -3x$ 　　　　 **2.** $x + y - 5 = 0$ 　　　　 **3.** $3x + y = 5$

4. $y = \dfrac{7}{3} - \dfrac{1}{3}x$ 　　　　 **5.** $y = 2$ 　　　　 **6.** $x + 4y - 4 = 0$

7. Which two lines in Exercises 1–6 are parallel? Explain.

NAME _____ DATE _____

Practice with Examples

For use with pages 242–251

EXAMPLE 2 *Graphing Using Slope and y-Intercept*

Graph the equation $5x - y = 3$.

SOLUTION

Write the equation in slope-intercept form: $y = 5x - 3$

Find the slope and the *y*-intercept: $m = 5$ and $b = -3$.

Plot the point $(0, b)$ when $b = -3$. Use the slope to locate a second point on the line.

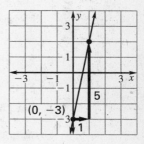

$$m = \frac{5}{1} = \frac{\text{rise}}{\text{run}} \rightarrow \frac{\text{move 5 units up}}{\text{move 1 unit right}}$$

Draw a line through the two points.

Exercises for Example 2

Write the equation in slope-intercept form. Then graph the equation.

8. $6x - y = 0$

9. $x + 3y - 3 = 0$

10. $5x + y = 4$

11. $x + 3y - 6 = 0$

12. $2x + y - 9 = 0$

13. $x + 2y + 8 = 0$

Algebra 1, Concepts and Skills
Practice Workbook with Examples

NAME _____ DATE _____

Practice with Examples

EXAMPLE 3 *Using a Linear Model*

During the summer you work for a lawn care service. You are paid $5 per day, plus an hourly rate of $1.50.

a. Using w to represent daily wages and h to represent the number of hours worked daily, write an equation that models your total wages for one day's work.

b. Find the slope and the y-intercept of the equation.

c. What does the slope represent?

d. Graph the equation, using the slope and the y-intercept.

SOLUTION

a. Using w to represent daily wages and h to represent the number of hours worked daily, the equation that models your total wages for one day's work is $w = 1.50h + 5$.

b. The slope of the equation is 1.50 and the y-intercept is 5.

c. The slope represents the hourly rate.

d.

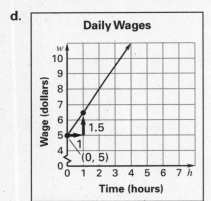

Exercises for Example 3

14. Rework Example 3 if you are paid $4 per day, plus an hourly rate of $1.75.

15. Rework Example 3 if you are paid $6 per day, plus an hourly rate of $1.25.

Algebra 1, Concepts and Skills
Practice Workbook with Examples

NAME _____ DATE _____

Practice with Examples

For use with pages 252–258

GOAL **Identify when a relation is a function and use function notation.**

> **VOCABULARY**
>
> A **relation** is any set of ordered pairs. A relation is a function if for each input there is exactly one output.
>
> Using **function notation,** the equation $y = 3x - 4$ becomes the function $f(x) = 3x - 4$ (the symbol $f(x)$ replaces y). Just as (x, y) is a solution of $y = 3x - 4$, $(x, f(x))$ is a solution of $f(x) = 3x - 4$.
>
> A function is called a **linear function** if it is of the form $f(x) = mx + b$.

EXAMPLE 1 *Identifying Functions*

Decide whether the relation shown in the input-output diagram is a function. If it is a function, give the domain and the range.

a. Input   Output

```
1 ——→ 4
2 ——→ 6
3 ——→ 8
4 ——→ 10
```

b. Input   Output

```
1 ——→ 5
2
3 ——→ 7
4
```

SOLUTION

a. The relation is not a function, because the input 3 has two outputs: 8 and 10.

b. The relation is a function. For each input there is exactly one output. The domain of the function is the set of input values 1, 2, 3, and 4. The range is the set of output values 5 and 7.

NAME _____ DATE _____

Practice with Examples

For use with pages 252–258

Exercises for Example 1

Decide whether the relation is a function. If it is a function, give the domain and the range.

1. Input   Output

$2 \longrightarrow 1$
$4 \longrightarrow 3$
$\quad \longrightarrow 5$
$8 \longrightarrow 7$

2. Input   Output

$1 \longrightarrow 1$
$2 \longrightarrow 4$
$3 \longrightarrow 9$
$4 \longrightarrow 16$

3. Input   Output

$1 \longrightarrow$
$2 \longrightarrow 4$
$3 \longrightarrow 6$
$4 \longrightarrow 8$

EXAMPLE 2 *Evaluating a Function*

Evaluate the function $f(x) = -4x + 5$ when $x = -1$.

SOLUTION

$$f(x) = -4x + 5 \qquad \text{Write original function.}$$
$$f(-1) = -4(-1) + 5 \qquad \text{Substitute } -1 \text{ for } x.$$
$$= 9 \qquad \text{Simplify.}$$

Exercises for Example 2

Evaluate the function when $x = 3$, $x = 0$, and $x = -2$.

4. $f(x) = 9x + 2$

5. $f(x) = 0.5x + 4$

6. $f(x) = -7x + 3$

Practice with Examples

For use with pages 252–258

EXAMPLE 3 *Graphing a Linear Function*

Graph $f(x) = \frac{3}{2}x - 2$..

SOLUTION

❶ **Rewrite** the function as $y = \frac{3}{2}x - 2$.

❷ **Find** the slope and the y-intercept.

$m = \frac{3}{2}$ and $b = -2$

❸ **Use** the slope to locate a second point.

❹ **Draw** a line through the two points.

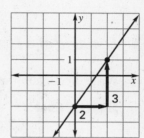

Exercises for Example 3

Graph the function.

7. $f(x) = 2x + 4$

8. $f(x) = -\frac{1}{3}x + 2$

9. $f(x) = -\frac{1}{2}x - 5$

NAME_____ DATE _____

Practice with Examples

For use with pages 269–275

GOAL **Use slope-intercept form to write an equation of a line.**

VOCABULARY

The **slope-intercept form** of the equation of a line with slope m and y-intercept b is $y = mx + b$.

EXAMPLE 1 *Equation of a Line*
_____

Write an equation of the line with slope 4 and y-intercept -3.

SOLUTION

$y = mx + b$ Write slope-intercept form.

$y = 4x + (-3)$ Substitute 4 for m and -3 for b.

$y = 4x - 3$ Simplify.

Exercises for Example 1
....

Write an equation of the line in slope-intercept form.

1. The slope is -2; the y-intercept is 5.

2. The slope is 1; the y-intercept is -4.

$$y = -2x + 5$$

$$y = 1x - 4$$

3. The slope is 0; the y-intercept is 2.

4. The slope is 3; the y-intercept is 6.

$$y = 2$$

$$y = 3x + 6$$

Algebra 1, Concepts and Skills
Practice Workbook with Examples

NAME _____ DATE _____

Practice with Examples

For use with pages 269–275

EXAMPLE 2 *Using a Graph to Write an Equation*

Write an equation of the line shown using slope-intercept form.

SOLUTION

Write the slope-intercept form $y = mx + b$.

Find the slope of the line. Let $(0, -2)$ be (x_1, y_1) and $(3, 0)$ be (x_2, y_2).

$$m = \frac{\text{rise}}{\text{run}} = \frac{y_2 - y_1}{x_2 - x_1} = \frac{0 - (-2)}{3 - 0} = \frac{2}{3}$$

Use the graph to find the y-intercept b. The y-intercept is -2.

Substitute $\frac{2}{3}$ for m and -2 for b in $y = mx + b$.

$$y = \frac{2}{3}x - 2$$

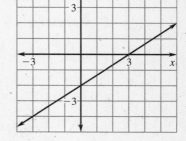

Exercises for Example 2

Write the equation of the line in slope-intercept form.

5.

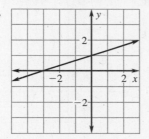

$$\frac{1}{-3}$$

6.

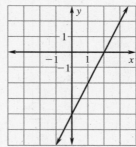
$$\frac{4}{2}$$

Practice with Examples

For use with pages 269–275

EXAMPLE 3 **Modeling Negative Slope**

Write an equation of the line shown using slope-intercept form.

SOLUTION

Write the slope-intercept form $y = mx + b$.

Find the slope of the line. Let $(0, 3)$ be (x_1, y_1) and $(1, 0)$ be (x_2, y_2).

$$m = \frac{\text{rise}}{\text{run}} = \frac{y_2 - y_1}{x_2 - x_1} = \frac{0 - 3}{1 - 0} = \frac{-3}{1} = -3$$

Use the graph to find the y-intercept b. The y-intercept is 3.

Substitute -3 for m and 3 for b in $y = mx + b$.

$$y = -3x + 3$$

Exercises for Example 3

Write the equation of the line in slope-intercept form.

7.

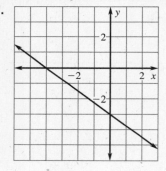

$$\frac{3}{-4}$$

8.

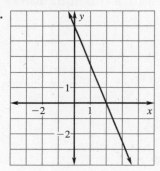

$$\frac{5}{2}$$

Practice with Examples

For use with pages 276–284

GOAL   **Use point-slope form to write the equation of a line.**

VOCABULARY

The **point-slope form** of the equation of the line through (x_1, y_1) with slope m is $y - y_1 = m(x - x_1)$.

EXAMPLE 1   *Using the Point-Slope Form*

Use the point-slope form of a line to write an equation of the line that passes through the point $(3, -1)$ and has a slope of -1.

SOLUTION

Use the slope of -1 and the point $(3, -1)$ as (x_1, y_1) in the point-slope form.

$$y - y_1 = m(x - x_1) \qquad \text{Write point-slope form.}$$
$$y - (-1) = -1(x - 3) \qquad \text{Substitute } -1 \text{ for } m, 3 \text{ for } x_1, \text{ and } -1 \text{ for } y_1.$$
$$y + 1 = -1(x - 3) \qquad \text{Simplify.}$$

Using the distributive property, you can write an equation in point-slope form in slope-intercept form.

$$y + 1 = -x + 3 \qquad \text{Use distributive property.}$$
$$y = -x + 2 \qquad \text{Subtract 1 from each side.}$$

NAME _____ DATE _____

Practice with Examples

For use with pages 276–284

Exercises for Example 1

Write in slope-intercept form the equation of the line that passes through the given point and has the given slope.

1. $(4, 5)$, $m = 2$

$$y - 5 = 2(x - 4)$$

2. $(-1, 6)$, $m = -3$

$$y - 6 = 3(x + 1)$$

3. $(-2, 8)$, $m = -4$

$$y - 8 = 4(x + 2)$$

Algebra 1, Concepts and Skills
Practice Workbook with Examples

Practice with Examples

For use with pages 276–284

EXAMPLE 2 *Writing an Equation of a Parallel Line*

Write in slope-intercept form the equation of the line that is parallel to the line $y = 3x - 5$ and passes through the point $(-5, -2)$.

SOLUTION

The slope of the original line is $m = 3$. So the slope of the parallel line is also $m = 3$. The line passes through the point $(x_1, y_1) = (-5, -2)$.

$y - y_1 = m(x - x_1)$	Write point-slope form.
$y - (-2) = 3(x - (-5))$	Substitute -2 for y_1, 3 for m, and -5 for x_1.
$y + 2 = 3(x + 5)$	Simplify.
$y + 2 = 3x + 15$	Use the distributive property.
$y = 3x + 13$	Subtract 2 from each side.

Exercises for Example 2

4. Write in slope-intercept form the equation of the line that is parallel to the line $y = -4x + 1$ and passes through the point $(2, -1)$.

$$Y + 1 = 4 \ (X_8 - 2)$$

5. Write in slope-intercept form the equation of the line that is parallel to the line $y = -x - 7$ and passes through the point $(-4, -4)$.

$$Y + 4 = -(x + 4)$$

NAME _____ DATE _____

Practice with Examples

For use with pages 285–290

GOAL **Write an equation of a line given two points on the line.**

EXAMPLE 1 *Writing an Equation Given Two Points*

Write an equation of the line that passes through the points $(1, 5)$ and $(2, 3)$.

SOLUTION

Find the slope of the line. Let $(x_1, y_1) = (1, 5)$ and $(x_2, y_2) = (2, 3)$.

$m = \dfrac{y_2 - y_1}{x_2 - x_1}$ Write formula for slope.

$\quad = \dfrac{3 - 5}{2 - 1}$ Substitute.

$\quad = \dfrac{-2}{1} = -2$ Simplify.

Write the equation of the line and let $m = -2$, $x_1 = 1$, and $y_1 = 5$ and solve for b.

$y - y_1 = m(x - x_1)$ Write point-slope form.

$y - 5 = -2(x - 1)$ Substitute -2 for m, 1 for x_1, and 5 for y_1.

$y = -2x + 7$ Distribute and simplify.

Exercises for Example 1

Write an equation in slope-intercept form of the line that passes through the points.

1. $(4, 9)$ and $(1, 6)$ **2.** $(0, 7)$ and $(1, -1)$ **3.** $(-2, -3)$ and $(0, 3)$

Algebra 1, Concepts and Skills
Practice Workbook with Examples

Practice with Examples

For use with pages 285–290

EXAMPLE 2 *Decide Which Form to Use*

Write the equation of the line in slope-intercept form.

a.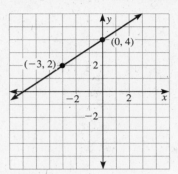

b.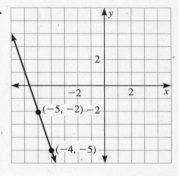

SOLUTION

a. Find the slope.

$$m = \frac{y_2 - y_1}{x_2 - x_1} = \frac{4 - 2}{0 - (-2)} = \frac{2}{3}$$

The y-intercept is $b = 4$.

$y = mx + b$

$y = \frac{2}{3}x + 4$

b. Find the slope.

$$m = \frac{y_2 - y_1}{x_2 - x_1} = \frac{-5 - (-2)}{-4 - (-5)} = \frac{-3}{1} = -3$$

Since you do not know the y-intercept, use the point slope form.

$y - y_1 = m(x - x_1)$

$y - (-2) = -3(x - (-5))$

$y - 2 = -3x - 15$

$y = -3x - 17$

NAME _____ DATE _____

Practice with Examples

For use with pages 285–290

Exercises for Example 2

Write the equation of the line in slope-intercept form.

4.

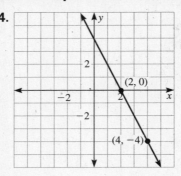

5.

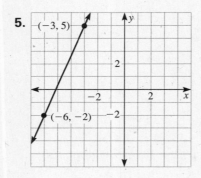

Algebra 1, Concepts and Skills
Practice Workbook with Examples

LESSON 5.4

Practice with Examples

For use with pages 291–297

GOAL **Write an equation of a line in standard form.**

VOCABULARY

The **standard form** of the equation of a line is $Ax + By = C$, where A and B are not both zero.

EXAMPLE 1 *Converting to Standard Form*

Write $y = -\frac{3}{4}x + 5$ in standard form with integer coefficients.

SOLUTION

To write the equation in standard form, isolate the variable terms on the left and the constant term on the right.

$$y = -\frac{3}{4}x + 5 \qquad \text{Write original equation.}$$
$$4y = 4\left(-\frac{3}{4}x + 5\right) \qquad \text{Multiply each side by 4.}$$
$$4y = -3x + 20 \qquad \text{Use distributive property.}$$
$$3x + 4y = 20 \qquad \text{Add } 3x \text{ to each side.}$$

Exercises for Example 1

Write the equation in standard form with integer coefficients.

1. $y = \frac{2}{3}x - 7$

2. $y = 8 + 2x$

3. $y = 6 - \frac{1}{4}x$

Algebra 1, Concepts and Skills
Practice Workbook with Examples

NAME _____ DATE _____

Practice with Examples
For use with pages 291–297

EXAMPLE 2 *Writing a Linear Equation in Standard Form*

Write the standard form of the equation passing through (3, 7) with a
slope of 2.

SOLUTION

Write the point-slope form of the equation of the line.

$y - y_1 = m(x - x_1)$	Write point-slope form.
$y - 7 = 2(x - 3)$	Substitute 7 for y_1, 2 for m, and 3 for x_1.
$y - 7 = 2x - 6$	Use distributive property.
$y = 2x + 1$	Add 7 to each side.
$-2x + y = 1$	Subtract $2x$ from each side.

Exercises for Example 2

**Write the standard form of the equation of the line that
passes through the given point and has the given slope.**

4. $(1, 4)$, $m = -2$

5. $(-3, 1)$, $m = 3$

6. $(5, -2)$, $m = -1$

Algebra 1, Concepts and Skills
Practice Workbook with Examples

Practice with Examples

For use with pages 291–297

EXAMPLE 3 *Writing an Equation in Standard Form*

A line passes through the points $(0, 2)$ and $(-4, -1)$. Write an equation of the line in standard form. Use integer coefficients.

❶ Find the slope. Use $(x_1, y_1) = (0, 2)$ and $(x_2, y_2) = (-4, -1)$.

$$m = \frac{y_2 - y_1}{x_2 - x_1}$$

$$= \frac{-1 - 2}{-4 - 0}$$

$$= \frac{-3}{-4} = \frac{3}{4}$$

❷ Write an equation of the line, using slope-intercept form.

$y = mx + b$	Write slope-intercept form.
$y = \dfrac{3}{4}x + 2$	Substitute $\dfrac{3}{4}$ for m and 2 for b.
$4y = 4\left(\dfrac{3}{4}x + 2\right)$	Multiply each side by 4.
	$4y = 3x + 8$ Use distributive property.
$-3x + 4y = 8$	Subtract $3x$ from each side.

Exercise for Example 3

7. Write in standard form an equation of the line that passes through the points $(1, 3)$ and $(0, 8)$. Use integer coefficients.

Algebra 1, Concepts and Skills
Practice Workbook with Examples

Practice with Examples

For use with pages 298–304

GOAL **Write and use a linear equation to solve a real-life problem.**

> **VOCABULARY**
>
> A **linear model** is a linear function that is used to model a real-life situation.
>
> A **rate of change** compares two quantities that are changing.

EXAMPLE 1 *Write a Linear Model*

In 1995 you had an investment worth $1000. It decreased in value by about $50 per year. Write a linear model for the value of your investment y. Let $t = 0$ represent 1995.

SOLUTION

The rate of decrease is $50 per year, so the slope is $m = -50$. The year 1995 is represented by $t = 0$. Therefore, the point (t_1, y_1) is (0, 1000).

$$y - y_1 = m(t - t_1) \qquad \text{Write the point-slope form.}$$
$$y - 1000 = -50(t - 0) \qquad \text{Substitute values.}$$
$$y - 1000 = -50t \qquad \text{Use the distributive property}$$
$$y = -50t + 1000 \qquad \text{Add 1000 to each side.}$$

Exercises for Example 1

1. You begin a hiking trail at 8:00 A.M. and hike at a rate of 3 miles per hour. Write a linear model for the number of miles hiked y. Let $t = 0$ represent 8:00 A.M.

2. You make an initial investment of $500 in 1995. It increases in value by about $100 per year. Write a linear model for the value of the investment in year t. Let $t = 0$ represent 1995.

Practice with Examples

For use with pages 298–304

EXAMPLE 2 *Use a Linear Model to Predict*

Use the linear model in Example 1 to predict the value of your
investment in 2003.

$y = -50t + 1000$	Write the linear model.
$y = -50(8) + 1000$	Substitute 8 for t.
$y = -400 + 1000$	Simplify.
$y = 600$	Solve for y.

In 2003 your investment will be worth $600.

Exercises for Example 2

3. Use the linear model you wrote in Exercise 1 to predict how many
miles you will have hiked at 10 A.M. if you continue at the same rate.

4. Use the linear model you wrote in Exercise 2 to predict the value of
your investment in 2001 if it increases at the same rate.

NAME _____ DATE _____

Practice with Examples

For use with pages 298–304

EXAMPLE 3 **Write and Use a Linear Model**

You are buying carrots and peas for dinner. The carrots cost $1.50 per pound and the peas cost $.75. You have $4.50 to spend.

a. Write an equation that models the different amounts (in pounds) of carrots and peas you can buy.

b. Use the model to complete the table that illustrates several different amounts of carrots and peas you can buy.

Carrots (lb), x	0	1	2	3
Peas (lb), y	?	?	?	?

SOLUTION

a. Let the amount of carrots (in pounds) be x and the amount of peas (in pounds) be y.

Verbal Model

Price of carrots	·	Weight of carrots	+	Price of peas	·	Weight of peas	=	Total cost

Labels   Price of carrots $= 1.5$ (dollars per pound)

Weight of carrots $= x$ (pounds)

Price of peas $= 0.75$ (dollars per pound)

Weight of peas $= y$ (pounds)

Total cost $= 4.50$ (dollars)

Algebraic Model $1.5x + 0.75y = 4.50$

b. Complete the table by substituting the given values of x into the equation $1.5x + 0.75y = 4.50$ to find y.

Carrots (lb), x	0	1	2	3
Peas (lb), y	6	4	2	?

Exercise for Example 3

5. You are buying jeans and shirts. You have $120. Jeans cost $40 and shirts cost $20. Write an equation that models the different amounts of jeans and shirts you can afford to buy. Use a table to show the different combinations of jeans and shirts you can buy.

Algebra 1, Concepts and Skills
Practice Workbook with Examples

NAME _____ DATE _____

Practice with Examples

For use with pages 305–312

GOAL **Write equations of perpendicular lines.**

EXAMPLE 1 *Identify Perpendicular Lines*

Determine whether the lines are perpendicular.

SOLUTION

The lines have slopes of 1 and −1.
Because $(1)(-1) = -1$, the lines
are perpendicular.

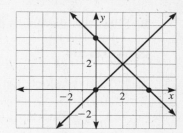

Exercises for Example 1

Determine whether the lines are perpendicular.

1. $y = -4x + 7, y = \frac{1}{4}x - 3$

2. $y = -\frac{2}{3}x + 3, y = -\frac{3}{2}x - 2$

Practice with Examples

For use with pages 305–312

EXAMPLE 2 *Show that Lines are Perpendicular*

a. Write in slope-intercept form the equation of the line passing through $(-2, 1)$ and $(6, -2)$.

b. Show that the line is perpendicular to the line $y = \dfrac{8}{3}x - 2$.

SOLUTION

a. 1. Find the slope. Let $(x_1, y_1) = (-2, 1)$ and $(x_2, y_2) = (6, -2)$.

$$m = \frac{y_2 - y_1}{x_2 - x_1} = \frac{-2 - 1}{6 - (-2)} = \frac{-3}{8} = -\frac{3}{8}$$

2. Write the equation of the line using point-slope form.

$$y - y_1 = m(x - x_1) \qquad \text{Write point-slope form.}$$

$$y - 1 = -\frac{3}{8}(x + 2) \qquad \text{Substitute } -\frac{3}{8} \text{ for } m, -2 \text{ for } x_1, \text{ and } 1 \text{ for } y_1.$$

$$y - 1 = -\frac{3}{8}x - \frac{3}{4} \qquad \text{Use distributive property.}$$

$$y = -\frac{3}{8}x + \frac{1}{4} \qquad \text{Add 1 to each side.}$$

b. The lines have slopes of $-\dfrac{3}{8}$ and $\dfrac{8}{3}$. Because $\left(-\dfrac{3}{8}\right)\left(\dfrac{8}{3}\right) = -1$, the lines are perpendicular.

Exercises for Example 2

3. Write in slope-intercept form the equation of the line passing through $(1, -3)$, and $(-2, -2)$. Show that the line is perpendicular to $y = 3x - 4$.

4. Write in slope-intercept form the equation of the line passing through $(-4, 6)$ and $(2, -3)$. Show that the line is perpendicular to $y = \dfrac{2}{3}x + 5$.

Practice with Examples

For use with pages 305–312

EXAMPLE 3 *Writing Equations of Perpendicular Lines*

Write an equation of the line that is perpendicular to the line
$y = -3x + 2$ and passes through the point $(6, 5)$.

SOLUTION

The given line has a slope of $m = -3$. A perpendicular line through
$(6, 5)$ must have a slope of $m = \frac{1}{3}$. Use this information to find the
y-intercept.

$y - y_1 = m(x - x_1)$ Write point-slope form.

$y - 5 = \frac{1}{3}(x - 6)$ Substitute $\frac{1}{3}$ for m, 6 for x_1, and 5 for y_1.

$y - 5 = \frac{1}{3}x - 2$ Use distributive property.

$y = \frac{1}{3}x + 3$ Add 5 to each side.

Exercises for Example 3

**Write an equation of the line that is perpendicular to the
given line and passes through the given point.**

5. $y = 2x - 1, \ (2, 4)$

6. $y = -\frac{1}{3}x + 2, \ (5, 1)$

7. $y = -4x + 5, \ (4, 3)$

NAME _____ DATE _____

Practice with Examples

For use with pages 323–328

GOAL Solve and graph one-step inequalities in one variable using addition or subtraction.

VOCABULARY

The **graph of an inequality** in one variable is the set of points on a number line that represent all solutions of the inequality.

Equivalent inequalities are inequalities that have the same solutions.

Addition property of inequality: For all real numbers

a, b, and c: If $a > b$, then $a + c > b + c$.
If $a < b$, then $a + c < b + c$.

Subtraction property of inequality: For all real numbers

a, b, and c: If $a > b$, then $a - c > b - c$.
If $a < b$, then $a - c < b - c$.

EXAMPLE 1 *Graphing an Inequality in One Variable*

---

a. Graph the inequality $3 > x$.

b. Graph the inequality $x \geq 4$.

SOLUTION

a. Notice that $3 > x$ gives the same information as $x < 3$. Use an open dot for the inequality symbol $<$ or $>$.

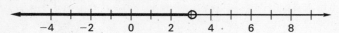

b. Use a closed dot for the inequality symbol $\leq$ or $\geq$.

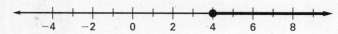

Exercises for Example 1

Graph the inequality.

1. $x \leq -1$

2. $x \geq 0$

3. $x < 0$

Practice with Examples

For use with pages 323–328

EXAMPLE 2 *Using Addition to Solve an Inequality*

Solve $x - 7 > -6$. Graph the solution.

SOLUTION

$$x - 7 > -6 \qquad \text{Write original inequality.}$$

$$x - 7 + 7 > -6 + 7 \qquad \text{Add 7 to each side.}$$

$$x > 1 \qquad \text{Simplify.}$$

The solution is all real numbers greater than 1. Check several numbers that are greater than 1 in the original inequality.

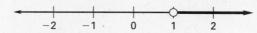

Exercises for Example 2

Solve the inequality and graph its solution.

4. $x - 5 < -9$

$$+5 \qquad +5$$

$$x < -4$$

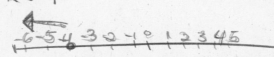

5. $a - 3 \le 0$

$$a \le 3$$

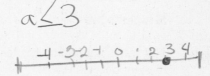

6. $t - 1 < -7$

$$+1$$

$$t < -6$$

Practice with Examples

For use with pages 323–328

EXAMPLE 3 *Use Subtraction to Solve an Inequality*

Solve $x + 2 < 7$. Graph the solution.

SOLUTION

$x + 2 < 7$	Write original inequality.
$x + 2 - 2 < 7 - 2$	Subtract 2 from each side.
$x < 5$	Simplify.

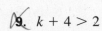

Exercises for Example 3

Solve the inequality and graph its solution.

7. $4 > y + 2$ **8.** $x + 3 \leq 0$ **9.** $k + 4 > 2$

EXAMPLE 4 *Write and Graph an Inequality in One Variable*

At sea level, water freezes at or below 0°C. Write and graph an inequality
that describes the freezing temperature.

SOLUTION

The water temperature is less than or equal to 0°C.
In symbols, $x \leq 0$.

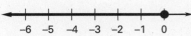

Exercise for Example 4

10. At sea level, ice melts at or above 32°F. Write and graph an inequality that describes
the melting temperature.

Practice with Examples

For use with pages 329–335

GOAL Solve and graph one-step inequalities in one variable using multiplication or division.

Multiplication property of inequality: For all real numbers a and b, and

for $c > 0$	for $c < 0$
If $a > b$, then $ac > bc$.	If $a > b$, then $ac < bc$.
If $a < b$, then $ac < bc$.	If $a < b$, then $ac > bc$.

Division property of inequality: For all real numbers a and b, and

for $c > 0$	for $c < 0$
If $a > b$, then $\dfrac{a}{c} > \dfrac{b}{c}$.	If $a > b$, then $\dfrac{a}{c} < \dfrac{b}{c}$.
If $a < b$, then $\dfrac{a}{c} < \dfrac{b}{c}$.	If $a < b$, then $\dfrac{a}{c} > \dfrac{b}{c}$.

EXAMPLE 1 *Multiply by a Positive Number*

a. Solve $\dfrac{x}{3} > 5$.   **b.** Solve $\dfrac{x}{2} \le -4$.

SOLUTION

a. $\dfrac{x}{3} > 5$

$3 \cdot \dfrac{x}{3} > 3 \cdot 5$

$x > 15$

b. $\dfrac{x}{2} \le -4$

$2 \cdot \dfrac{x}{2} \le 2 \cdot (-4)$

$x \le -8$

Exercises for Example 1

Solve the inequality and graph its solution.

1. $\dfrac{x}{-4} < -2 \cdot 4$

$x < -8$

2. $\dfrac{t}{2} > 3 \cdot 2$

$+76$

3. $\dfrac{b}{5} \ge -3 \cdot 3$

$b \ge -15$

Practice with Examples

For use with pages 329–335

EXAMPLE 2 *Divide by a Positive Number*

a. Solve $2x < -4$.

b. Solve $3x \geq 15$.

SOLUTION

a. $2x < -4$

$$\frac{2x}{2} < \frac{-4}{2}$$

$$x < -2$$

b. $3x \geq 15$

$$\frac{3x}{3} \geq \frac{15}{3}$$

$$x \geq 5$$

Exercises for Example 2

Solve the inequality and graph its solution.

4. $\dfrac{6a}{6} > \dfrac{36}{6}$

$a > 6$

5. $\dfrac{4x}{4} \leq \dfrac{-16}{4}$

$x \leq -4$

6. $\dfrac{7y}{7} \leq \dfrac{-21}{7}$

$y \leq -3$

Algebra 1, Concepts and Skills
Practice Workbook with Examples

NAME _____ DATE _____

Practice with Examples

For use with pages 329–335

EXAMPLE 3 *Multiply by a Negative Number*

a. Solve $-\dfrac{n}{2} < 5$.   **b.** Solve $-\dfrac{t}{3} \geq -1$.

SOLUTION

When you multiply each side of an inequality by a negative number, you must change the direction of the inequality symbol.

a. $\qquad -\dfrac{n}{2} < 5.$

$$-2 \cdot -\dfrac{n}{2} > -2 \cdot 5$$

$$n > -10$$

b. $\qquad -\dfrac{t}{3} \geq -1.$

$$-3 \cdot -\dfrac{t}{3} \leq -3 \cdot (-1)$$

$$t \leq 3$$

Exercises for Example 3

Solve the inequality and graph its solution.

7. $-\dfrac{1}{2}x > 2$ $x < 4$

8. $-\dfrac{y}{5} < -2$ $y > -10$

9. $-\dfrac{z}{2} \leq 3$ $z \geq 6$

EXAMPLE 4 *Divide by a Negative Number*

a. Solve $-4n > 20$.   **b.** Solve $-6n < -24$.

SOLUTION

When you divide each side of an inequality by a negative number, you must change the direction of the inequality symbol.

a. $-4n > 20$

$$\dfrac{-4n}{-4} < \dfrac{20}{-4}$$

$$n < -5$$

b. $-6n < -24$

$$\dfrac{-6n}{-6} > \dfrac{-24}{-6}$$

$$n > 4$$

Exercises for Example 4

Solve the inequality and graph its solution.

10. $-2n \leq 12$ $\dfrac{-2n}{2}$ -5 $n \geq -6$

11. $-8p > 32$ $\dfrac{-8p}{-8}$ $\dfrac{32}{8}$ $p < 4$

12. $-9q \geq -27$ $\dfrac{-9q}{-9}$ $\dfrac{-27}{-9}$ $q \leq 3$

Practice with Examples

For use with pages 336–341

GOAL Solve multi-step linear inequalities in one variable.

EXAMPLE 1 *Using More than One Step*

Solve $3n + 2 \leq 14$.

SOLUTION

$3n + 2 \leq 14$	Write original inequality.
$3n \leq 12$	Subtract 2 from each side.
$n \leq 4$	Divide each side by 3.

The solution is all real numbers less than or equal to 4.

Exercises for Example 1

Solve the inequality.

1. $5x - 7 > -2$
$+7 \quad +7$

$$\frac{5x}{5} > \frac{5}{5}$$

$$x > 1$$

2. $9m + 2 \leq 20$
$-2 \quad -2$

$$\frac{9m}{9} \leq \frac{15}{9}$$

$$m \leq 2$$

3. $13 + 4y \geq 9$
$-13 \quad -13$

$$\frac{4y}{4} \geq \frac{4}{4}$$

$$4y > 1$$

$$y > 1$$

EXAMPLE 2 *Use the Distributive Property*

Solve $4(x - 1) > 8$.

SOLUTION

$4(x - 1) > 8$	Write original inequality.
$4x - 4 > 8$	Use distributive property.
$4x > 12$	Add 4 to each side.
$x > 3$	Divide each side by 4.

Practice with Examples

For use with pages 336–341

Exercises for Example 2

Solve the inequality.

4. $2(x - 2) < -14$

$2x - 4 < -14$
$\quad +4 \quad +4$

$\dfrac{2x}{2} < \dfrac{-10}{2}$

$x < -5$

5. $-5(x + 3) \leq -45$

$-5x - 15 \leq -45$
$\quad +15 \quad +15$

$\dfrac{-5x}{-5} \leq \dfrac{-30}{-5}$

$x \leq 6$

6. $3(-y + 2) \geq -12$

$-3y + 6 \geq -12$
$\quad -6 \quad -6$

$\dfrac{-3y}{-3} \geq \dfrac{-18}{-3}$

$y \leq 6$

EXAMPLE 3 **Collect Variable Terms**

Solve $11 - 2x \geq 3x + 16$.

SOLUTION

$11 - 2x \geq 3x + 16$	Write original inequality.
$-2x \geq 3x + 5$	Subtract 11 from each side.
$-5x \geq 5$	Subtract $3x$ from each side.
$x \leq -1$	Divide each side by -5 and reverse inequality.

The solution is all real numbers less than or equal to -1.

Exercises for Example 3

Solve the inequality.

7. $2a + 8 > 5 + a$
$\quad -8 \quad -8$

$a > -3$

8 $4y - 3 > 2y + 9$
$\quad +3 \quad +3$

$\dfrac{2y}{2} > \dfrac{12}{2}$

$\boxed{y > 6}$

9. $5z + 1 \geq 2z + 13$
$\quad -1 \quad -1$

$5z$
$\dfrac{3z}{3} \geq \dfrac{12}{3}$

$z \geq 4$

Algebra 1, Concepts and Skills
Practice Workbook with Examples

NAME _____ DATE _____

Practice with Examples

For use with pages 336–341

EXAMPLE 4 ·*Writing and Using a Linear Model*

You have $25 saved toward a new snowboard. You are also saving your earnings from a dishwashing job that pays $5.15 per hour. How many hours must you work before you have at least $225 saved?

SOLUTION

| **Verbal Model** | Hourly wage | · | Number of hours worked | + | Money already saved | ≥ | Desired savings |

Labels

Hourly wage = 5.15   (dollars per hour)

Number of hours worked = x (hours)

Money already saved = 25   (dollars)

Desired savings = 225   (dollars)

Algebraic Model

$5.15x + 25 \geq 225$ Write algebraic model.

$5.15x \geq 200$ Subtract 25 from each side.

$\dfrac{5.15x}{5.15} \geq \dfrac{200}{5.15}$ Divide each side by 5.15.

$x \geq 38.835\ldots$

You need to work at least 39 hours.

Exercises for Example 4

10. Rework Example 4 if you earn $5.60 per hour and have $30 saved.

11. Rework Example 4 if you need to have at least $265 saved.

Algebra 1, Concepts and Skills
Practice Workbook with Examples

Practice with Examples

For use with pages 342–347

GOAL Solve and graph compound inequalities involving *and*.

> ### VOCABULARY
>
> A **compound inequality** consists of two inequalities connected by *and* or *or*.

EXAMPLE 1 *Writing Compound Inequalities with And*

Write an inequality that represents all real numbers that are greater than or equal to −2 *and* less than 1. Graph the inequality.

SOLUTION

$-2 \leq x < 1$

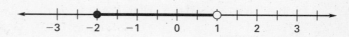

Exercises for Example 1

Write an inequality that represents the statement and graph the inequality.

1. *x* is greater than −4 *and* less than or equal to −2.

$$-4 < x \leq -2$$

2. *x* is greater than −3 *and* less than −1.

$$-3 < x < -1$$

EXAMPLE 2 *Compound Inequalities in Real Life*

In 1985, a real estate property was sold for $145,000. The property was sold again in 1999 for $211,000. Write a compound inequality that represents the different values that the property was worth between 1985 and 1999.

SOLUTION

Use the variable *v* to represent the property value. Write a compound inequality to represent the different property values.

$$145,000 \leq v \leq 211,000$$

Practice with Examples

For use with pages 342–347

Exercise for Example 2

3. Rework Example 2 if the property was sold in 1985 for \$172,000 and was sold again in 1999 for \$226,000.

EXAMPLE 3 *Solve Compound Inequalities with And*

Solve $-4 \le x - 3 < 6$. Then graph.

SOLUTION

Isolate the variable x between the two inequality symbols.

$$-4 \le x - 3 < 6 \qquad \text{Write original inequality.}$$

$$-1 \le x < 9 \qquad \text{Add 3 to each expression.}$$

The solution is all real numbers greater than or equal to -1 *and* less than 9.

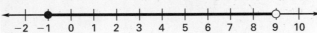

Exercises for Example 3

Solve the inequality and graph the solution.

4. $5 \le x + 7 \le 9$

$-7 -7 -7$

$-2 \le x \le 2$

5. $-6 < x - 4 \le 7$

$+4 +4 +4$

$-2 < x \le 11$

6. $0 \le x - 3 < 10$

$+3 +3 +3$

$3 \le x < 13$

Algebra 1, Concepts and Skills
Practice Workbook with Examples

Practice with Examples

For use with pages 342–347

EXAMPLE 4 ___ *Solve Multi-Step Compound Inequalities*

Solve $-9 \le -4x - 5 < 3$. Graph the solution.

SOLUTION

Isolate the variable x between the two inequality symbols.

$-9 \le -4x - 5 < 3$	Write original inequality.
$-4 \le -4x < 8$	Add 5 to each expression.
$1 \ge x > -2$	Divide each expression by -4 and *reverse* both inequality symbols.

The solution is all real numbers that are less than or equal to 1 *and* greater than -2.

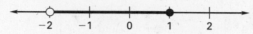

Exercises for Example 4

Solve the inequality and graph the solution.

7. $-3 < 2x + 1 \le 7$

$\quad -1 \qquad\qquad -1\ -1$

$\quad \dfrac{-4}{2} < \dfrac{2x}{2} \le \dfrac{6}{2} \qquad -2 < x \le 3$

8. $-9 < -3 + 2x < -5$

$\quad +3\ +3 \qquad\qquad +3$

$\quad \dfrac{-6}{2} < \dfrac{2x}{2} < \dfrac{2}{2}$

$\qquad\qquad -3 < x < 1$

9. $2 \le -3x + 8 < 17$

$\quad -8 \qquad -8\ -8$

$\quad \dfrac{-6}{3} \le \dfrac{-3x}{-3} < \dfrac{9}{-3} \qquad 2 \le x < -3$

Practice with Examples

For use with pages 348–353

GOAL Solve and graph compound inequalities involving *or*.

EXAMPLE 1 *Writing Compound Inequalities with Or*

Write an inequality that represents all real numbers that are less than 0 *or* greater than 3. Graph the inequality.

SOLUTION

$x < 0$ *or* $x > 3$

Exercises for Example 1

Write an inequality that represents the statement and graph the inequality.

1. All real numbers less than -4 *or* greater than or equal to -2

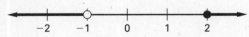

2. All real numbers greater than 3 *or* less than -1

$x > 3 < -1$

EXAMPLE 2 *Solving a Multi-Step Inequality with Or*

Solve $5x + 1 < -4$ *or* $6x - 2 \geq 10$. Graph the solution.

SOLUTION

You can solve each part separately.

$$5x + 1 < -4 \quad or \quad 6x - 2 \geq 10$$
$$5x < -5 \quad or \quad 6x \geq 12$$
$$x < -1 \quad or \quad x \geq 2$$

The solution is all real numbers that are less than -1 *or* greater than or equal to 2.

NAME _____ DATE _____

Practice with Examples

For use with pages 348–353

Exercises for Example 2

Solve the inequality and graph the solution.

3. $2x - 3 < 5$ *or* $3x + 1 \geq 16$

$$\frac{2x}{2} < \frac{8}{2} \qquad \frac{3x}{3} > \frac{15}{3}$$

$$x < 4 \text{ or } x > 5$$

4. $-4x + 2 < 6$ *or* $2x \leq -6$

$$\frac{-4x}{-4} < \frac{4}{-4} \qquad x \leq -3$$

$$x < -1 \text{ or } x \leq -3$$

EXAMPLE 3 | *Solving a Compound Inequality with Or*

Solve $x - 1 \leq -3$ *or* $x + 3 > 6$. Graph the solution.

SOLUTION

$$x - 1 \leq -3 \qquad or \qquad x + 3 > 6$$
$$x \leq -2 \qquad or \qquad x > 3$$

Exercises for Example 3

Solve the inequality and graph the solution.

5. $x + 2 < -4$ *or* $x - 3 \geq 0$

$$x < -6 \text{ or } x \geq 3$$

6. $x + 1 < 1$ *or* $x - 4 > 1$

$$x < 0 \text{ or } x > 5$$

Algebra 1, Concepts and Skills
Practice Workbook with Examples

Practice with Examples

For use with pages 348–353

EXAMPLE 4 **Reverse Both Inequalities**

Solve $-x + 3 < -2 \ or \ -4 -x > 5$. Graph the solution.

SOLUTION

$$-x + 3 < -2 \qquad or \qquad -4 -x > 5$$
$$-3 - x + 3 < -2 - 3 \qquad or \qquad -4 - x + 4 > 5 + 4$$
$$-x < -5 \qquad or \qquad -x > 9$$
$$(-1)(-x) > -5(-1) \qquad or \qquad (-1)(-x) < 9(-1)$$
$$x > 5 \qquad or \qquad x < -9$$

Exercises for Example 4

Solve the inequality and graph the solution.

7. $-x + 5 < -1 \ or \ -x - 3 > 7$

$$\begin{array}{cc} -5 \quad -5 & +3 \end{array}$$

$$x > +6 \quad or \quad x < -10$$

8. $-x - 1 \le 2 \ or \ -x + 2 > 7$

$$+ (-1$$

$$-x \le 3 \quad or \quad \dfrac{-x > 5}{}$$

$$x \ge -3 \ or \ x < -5$$

Algebra 1, Concepts and Skills
Practice Workbook with Examples

NAME _____ DATE _____

Practice with Examples

For use with pages 354–360

GOAL **Solve absolute-value equations in one variable.**

> **VOCABULARY**
>
> An **absolute-value equation** is an equation of the form $|ax + b| = c$.

EXAMPLE 1 *Solving an Absolute-Value Equation*

a. Solve $|x| = 4$.   **b.** Solve $|x| = -5$.

SOLUTION

a. $|x| = 4$
    $x = 4$ or $x = -4$

b. $|x| = -5$

The absolute value of a number is never negative. The equation $|x| = -5$ has no solution.

Exercises for Example 1

Solve the equation.

1. $|x| = 8$ **2.** $|x| = -2$ **3.** $|x| = 6$

$-8\,8$ $2,-2$ $6,-6$

EXAMPLE 2 *Solving an Absolute-Value Equation*

Solve $|x - 3| = 4$.

SOLUTION
    $|x - 3| = 4$

The expression $x - 3$ can equal 4 or -4.
      $x - 3 = 4$ or $x - 3 = -4$
         $x = 7$ or $x = -1$

Exercises for Example 2

Solve the absolute-value equation.

4. $|x + 6| = 8$ **5.** $|x - 1| = 8$ **6.** $|x + 3| = 11$

                               $+1\ +1$ -3

$x = 2$ $x = -14$ $x = 9$ $x = -7$ $x = 8$

                                                       $x = -14$

NAME _____ DATE _____

Practice with Examples

For use with pages 354–360

EXAMPLE 3 *Solving an Absolute-Value Equation*

Solve $|4x + 2| = 18$.

SOLUTION

Because $|4x + 2| = 18$, the expression $4x + 2$ can be equal to 18 or -18.

$4x + 2$ IS POSITIVE	$4x + 2$ IS NEGATIVE
$|4x + 2| = 18$	$|4x + 2| = 18$
$4x + 2 = +18$	$4x + 2 = -18$
$4x = 16$	$4x = -20$
$x = 4$	$x = -5$

The equation has two solutions: 4 and -5.

Exercises for Example 3

Solve the equation.

7. $|2x + 1| = 15$

$$\frac{2x}{2} = \frac{14}{2} \quad x = 7$$
$$x = -8$$

8. $|2x - 6| = 8$

$$\frac{2x}{2} = \frac{14}{2}$$
$$\boxed{x = 7} \qquad \frac{2x}{2} = \frac{2}{2}$$
$$\boxed{x = -1}$$

9. $|2x - 3| = 9$

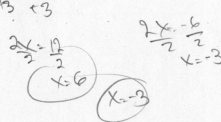

$$\frac{2x}{2} = \frac{12}{2} \qquad \frac{2x}{2} = \frac{-6}{2}$$
$$\boxed{x = 6} \qquad x = -3$$
$$\boxed{x = -3}$$

Algebra 1, Concepts and Skills
Practice Workbook with Examples

Practice with Examples

For use with pages 354–360

EXAMPLE 4 **Write an Absolute-Value Equation**

Write an absolute-value equation that has 4 and 8 as its solutions.

SOLUTION

The midpoint between 4 and 8 is 6.

The distance of the midpoint from the solutions is 2.

$$|x - 6| = 2$$
Midpoint **Distance**

Answer: $|x - 6| = 2$

Exercises for Example 4

10. Write an absolute-value equation that has -2 and 6 as its solutions.

Practice with Examples

For use with pages 361–366

GOAL **Solve absolute value inequalities in one variable.**

> ### VOCABULARY
>
> An **absolute-value inequality** is an inequality that has one of these forms:
>
> $$|ax + b| < c \qquad |ax + b| \le c \qquad |ax + b| > c \qquad |ax + b| \ge c$$

EXAMPLE 1 *Solving an Absolute-Value Inequality*

Solve and graph $|x| > 3$.

SOLUTION

$x > 3$ or $x < -3$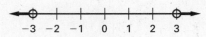

Exercises for Example 1

Solve the inequality.

1. $|x| > 4$

$x > 4 \quad x < -4$

2. $|x| > -2$

$x > -2 \quad x < 2$

3. $|x| > 1$

$x > 1 \quad x < -1$

EXAMPLE 2 *Solving an Absolute-Value Inequality*

Solve $|x + 5| \le 1$.

SOLUTION

The solution consists of all numbers x whose distance from -5 is less than or equal to 1. The inequality involves $\le$ so the related inequalities are connected by *and*.

$$|x + 5| \le 1$$

$$x + 5 \le 1 \qquad and \qquad x + 5 \ge -1$$
$$x \le -4 \qquad and \qquad x \ge -6$$

The solution is all real numbers greater than or equal to -6 *and* less than or equal to -4, which can be written as $-6 \le x \le -4$.

Practice with Examples

For use with pages 361–366

Exercises for Example 2

Solve the inequality.

4. $|x - 3| < 2$

$+3 \quad +3$

$x < 5$

$x > 1$

5. $|8 + x| \leq 3$

-8

$x < -3$

$x \geq$

6. $|x - 1.5| < 1$

EXAMPLE 3 *Solving an Absolute-Value Inequality*

Solve $|2x - 1| > 5$.

SOLUTION

When an absolute value is *greater than* a number, the related inequalities are connected by *or*.

$$|2x - 1| > 5$$

$$2x - 1 > 5 \qquad or \qquad 2x - 1 < -5$$
$$2x > 6 \qquad or \qquad 2x < -4$$
$$x > 3 \qquad or \qquad x < -2$$

The solution of $|2x - 1| > 5$ is all real numbers greater than 3 *or* less than -2, which can be written as the compound inequality $x < -2$ *or* $x > 3$.

Exercises for Example 3

Solve the inequality.

7. $|x + 2| \geq 1$

$-2 \quad -2$

$x \geq -1$

$x \leq -3$

8. $|x - 4| \geq 2$

$+4 +4$

$x \geq 6$

$x \leq 2$

9. $|2x + 1| > -3$

-1

$\dfrac{2x}{2} > \dfrac{2}{2}$

$x > 1$

$x < -4$

Algebra 1, Concepts and Skills
Practice Workbook with Examples

Practice with Examples

For use with pages 361–366

EXAMPLE 4 *Solve a Multi-Step Absolute-Value Inequality*

Solve the inequality $|x - 4| + 3 < 8$.

SOLUTION

First isolate the absolute-value expression on one side of the inequality.

$|x - 4| + 3 < 8$

$|x - 4| + 3 - 3 < 8 - 3$

$|x - 4| < 5$

$x - 4 < 5$ *and* $x - 4 > -5$

$x < 9$ *and* $x > -1$

This can be written $-1 < x < 9$.

Exercises for Example 4

Solve the absolute-value inequality.

10. $|x - 3| + 1 \leq 6$

$-1\ -1$

$x-3 \leq 5$

$+3\ +3$

$x \leq 8$

11. $|x + 2| - 4 > 8$

$+4\ +4$

$x + 2 > 12$

-2

$x > 10$

Algebra 1, Concepts and Skills
Practice Workbook with Examples

NAME _____ DATE _____

Practice with Examples

For use with pages 367–374

GOAL **Graph a linear inequality in two variables.**

> **VOCABULARY**
>
> A **linear inequality** in x and y is an inequality that can be written as $ax + by < c$, $ax + by \leq c$, $ax + by > c$, or $ax + by \geq c$, where a, b, and c are given numbers.

EXAMPLE 1 *Checking Solutions of a Linear Inequality*

Check whether the ordered pair is a solution of $3x - y \geq 2$.

a. $(0, 0)$ **b.** $(2, 0)$ **c.** $(2, 3)$

SOLUTION

(x, y)	$3x - y \geq 2$	**Conclusion**
a. $(0, 0)$	$3(0) - 0 = 0 \not\geq 2$	$(0, 0)$ is not a solution.
b. $(2, 0)$	$3(2) - 0 = 6 \geq 2$	$(2, 0)$ is a solution.
c. $(2, 3)$	$3(2) - 3 = 3 \geq 2$	$(2, 3)$ is a solution.

Exercises for Example 1

Is each ordered pair a solution of the inequality?

1. $x + 2y < 0$; $(0, 0), (-1, -2)$

Not a solution

2. $2x + y > 3$; $(2, 2), (-2, 2)$

Is a solution

NAME _____ DATE _____

Practice with Examples

For use with pages 367–374

EXAMPLE 2 *Vertical and Horizontal lines*

Graph the inequality.

a. $x \geq -2$ **b.** $y < -3$

SOLUTION

a. Graph the corresponding equation $x = -2$. The graph is a vertical line. The points on the line are solutions, so use a solid line.

The origin, (0, 0), is a solution since $0 \geq -2$. Shade the region that includes the origin—the points to the right of the line.

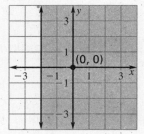

b. Graph the corresponding equation $y = -3$. The graph is a horizontal line. The points on the line are not solutions, so use a dashed line.

The origin, (0, 0), is not a solution since $0 > -3$. Shade the region that does not include the origin—the points below the line.

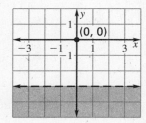

Exercises for Example 2

Graph the inequality.

3. $x \leq 2$

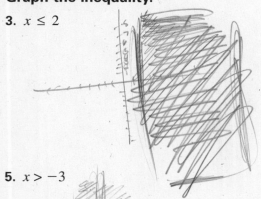

4. $y > -1$

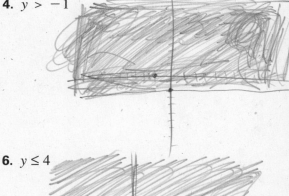

5. $x > -3$

6. $y \leq 4$

Algebra 1, Concepts and Skills
Practice Workbook with Examples

Practice with Examples

For use with pages 367–374

EXAMPLE 3 *Graphing a Linear Inequality in Two Variables*

Graph $x - y < 2$.

SOLUTION

The corresponding equation is $x - y = 2$. To graph this line, first write the equation in slope-intercept form: $y = x - 2$.

Graph the line that has a slope of 1 and a y-intercept of -2. Use a dashed line to show that the points on the line are not solutions.

The origin $(0, 0)$ is a solution and it lies above the line. So, the graph of $x - y < 2$ is all points above the line $y = x - 2$.

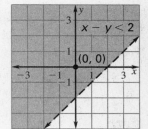

Exercises for Example 3

Graph the inequality.

7. $y - x < 3$

$y = x - 3$

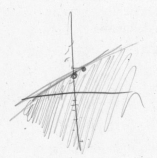

8. $2x + y \geq 4$

$y = 2x - 4$

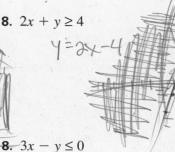

9. $x + y > -2$

$y = x + 2$

8. $3x - y \leq 0$

$y \leq -3x$

Practice with Examples

For use with pages 389–395

GOAL **Estimate the solution of a system of linear equations by graphing.**

> ### VOCABULARY
>
> Two or more linear equations in the same variables form a **system of linear equations** or simply a **linear system.**
>
> A **solution of a system of linear equations** in two variables is a pair of numbers a and b for which $x = a$ and $y = b$ make each equation a true statement.
>
> The point (a, b) lies on the graph of each equation and is the **point of intersection** of the graphs.

EXAMPLE 1 *Graph and Check a Linear System*

Solve the linear system graphically. Check the solution algebraically.

$$-3x + y = -7 \qquad \text{Equation 1}$$
$$2x + 2y = 10 \qquad \text{Equation 2}$$

SOLUTION

Write each equation in slope-intercept form.

$$y = 3x - 7 \qquad \text{Slope: 3, } y\text{-intercept: } -7$$
$$y = -x + 5 \qquad \text{Slope: } -1, y\text{-intercept: 5}$$

Graph each equation. The lines appear to intersect at $(3, 2)$.

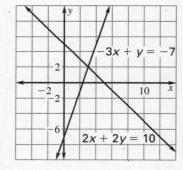

To check $(3, 2)$ as a solution algebraically, substitute 3 for x and 2 for y in each original equation.

EQUATION 1	EQUATION 2
$-3x + y = -7$	$2x + 2y = 10$
$-3(3) + 2 \overset{?}{=} -7$	$2(3) + 2(2) \overset{?}{=} 10$
$-7 = -7$	$10 = 10$

Because $(3, 2)$ is a solution of each equation in the linear system, it is a solution of the linear system.

NAME _M&on Herod_ DATE _____

Practice with Examples

For use with pages 389–395

Exercises for Example 1

Estimate the solution of the linear system graphically. Then check the solution algebraically.

1. $y = -x + 5$
   $y = x + 1$

2. $2x - y = 2$
   $x = 4$

$y = 2x - 2$

$x \cdot 4$

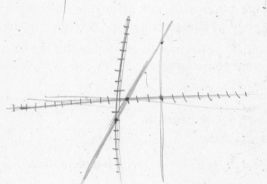

3. $2x + y = 2$
   $x - y = 4$

EXAMPLE 2 *Using a Linear System to Model a Real-Life Problem*

Tickets for the theater are $5 for the balcony and $10 for the orchestra. If 600 tickets were sold and the total receipts were $4750, how many tickets of each type were sold?

SOLUTION

Verbal Model

Number of balcony tickets	+	Number of orchestra tickets	=	Total number of tickets

Price of balcony tickets	·	Number of balcony tickets	+	

Price of orchestra tickets	·	Number of orchestra tickets	=	Total receipts

(continued)

Practice with Examples

For use with pages 389–395

Labels Price of balcony tickets $= 5$ (dollars)

Number of balcony tickets $= x$ (tickets)

Price of orchestra tickets $= 10$ (dollars)

Number of orchestra tickets $= y$ (tickets)

Total number of tickets $= 600$ (tickets)

Total receipts $= 4750$ (dollars)

Algebraic $x + y = 600$ Equation 1 (tickets)

Model $5x + 10y = 4750$ Equation 2 (receipts)

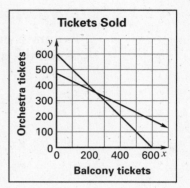

Tickets Sold

Use the graph-and-check method to solve the system.
The point of intersection of the two lines appears to be (250, 350).

According to the model, 250 tickets for the balcony and 350 tickets for
the orchestra were sold.

Exercises for Example 2

4. Algebraically check the solution for Example 2.

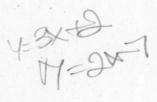

5. Rework Example 2 if 800 tickets were sold.

6. Rework Example 2 if total receipts were $3500.

NAME _____ DATE _____

Practice with Examples

For use with pages 396–401

GOAL **Solve a linear system by substitution.**

EXAMPLE 1 ***The Substitution Method***

Solve the linear system. $x + y = 1$ Equation 1

$2x - 3y = 12$ Equation 2

SOLUTION

Solve for y in Equation 1.

$y = -x + 1$ Revised Equation 1

Substitute $-x + 1$ for y in Equation 2 and solve for x.

$2x - 3y = 12$	Write Equation 2.
$2x - 3(-x + 1) = 12$	Substitute $-x + 1$ for y.
$2x + 3x - 3 = 12$	Distribute the -3.
$5x - 3 = 12$	Combine like terms.
$5x = 15$	Add 3 to each side.
$x = 3$	Divide each side by 5.

To find the value of y, substitute 3 for x in the revised Equation 1.

$y = -x + 1$	Write revised Equation 1.
$y = -3 + 1$	Substitute 3 for x.
$y = -2$	Solve for y.

The solution is $(3, -2)$.

Practice with Examples

For use with pages 396–401

Exercises for Example 1

Use the substitution method to solve the linear system.

1. $x + 2y = -5$
   $4x - 3y = 2$

2. $3x - 2y = 4$
   $x + 3y = 5$

3. $3x + y = -2$
   $x + 3y = 2$

EXAMPLE 2 *Writing and Using a Linear System*

An investor bought 225 shares of stock, stock A at $50 per share and stock B at $75 per share. If $13,750 worth of stock was purchased, how many shares of each kind did the investor buy?

SOLUTION

Verbal Model

Amount of stock A	+	Amount of stock B	=	Total amount of stock

Price of stock A	·	Amount of stock A	+	Price of stock B	·	Amount of stock B	=	Total investment

Labels

Amount of stock A = x (shares)

Amount of stock B = y (shares)

Total amount of stock = 225   (shares)

Price of stock A = 50   (dollars per share)

Price of stock B = 75   (dollars per share)

Total investment = 13,750   (dollars)

(continued)

Practice with Examples

For use with pages 396–401

Algebraic	$x + y = 225$	Equation 1 (shares)
Model	$50x + 75y = 13{,}750$	Equation 2 (dollars)

Solve for y in Equation 1.

$y = -x + 225$ Revised Equation 1

Substitute $-x + 225$ for y in Equation 2 and solve for x.

$50x + 75y = 13{,}750$	Write Equation 2.
$50x + 75(-x + 225) = 13{,}750$	Substitute $-x + 225$ for y.
$50x - 75x + 16{,}875 = 13{,}750$	Distribute the 75.
$-25x = -3125$	Simplify.
$x = 125$	Solve for x.

To find the value of y, substitute 125 for x in the revised Equation 1.

$y = -x + 225$	Write revised Equation 1.
$y = -125 + 225$	Substitute 125 for x.
$y = 100$	Solve for y.

The solution is (125, 100).

The investor bought 125 shares of stock A and 100 shares of stock B.

Exercises for Example 2

4. Rework Example 2 if the investor bought 200 shares of stock.

5. Rework Example 2 if $16,250 worth of stock was purchased.

Practice with Examples

For use with pages 402–408

GOAL Solve a system of linear equations by linear combinations.

VOCABULARY

A **linear combination** of two equations is an equation obtained by
(1) multiplying one or both equations by a constant if necesssary and
(2) adding the resulting equations.

EXAMPLE 1 *Multiply Then Add*

Solve the linear system. $4x - 3y = 11$ Equation 1

$3x + 2y = -13$ Equation 2

SOLUTION

The equations are arranged with like terms in columns. You can get the
coefficients of y to be opposites by multiplying the first equation by 2
and the second equation by 3.

$4x - 3y = 11$ Multiply by 2. $8x - 6y = 22$

$3x + 2y = -13$ Multiply by 3. $\underline{9x + 6y = -39}$

$17x = -17$ Add the equations.

$x = -1$ Solve for x.

Substitute -1 for x in the second equation and solve for y.

$3x + 2y = -13$ Write Equation 2.

$3(-1) + 2y = -13$ Substitute -1 for x.

$-3 + 2y = -13$ Simplify.

$y = -5$ Solve for y.

The solution is $(-1, -5)$.

Exercises for Example 1

Use linear combinations to solve the system of linear equations.

1. $5x + 2y = 1$

$-5x + 2y = 1$

2. $-7x + 2y = 4$

$7x + 2y = 4$

Algebra 1, Concepts and Skills
Practice Workbook with Examples

NAME _____ DATE _____

Practice with Examples

For use with pages 402–408

Use linear combinations to solve the system of linear equations.

3. $4x - 3y = 9$
  $x + 3y = 6$

4. $x + 2y = 5$
  $3x - 2y = 7$

5. $x + y = 1$
  $2x - 3y = 12$

6. $x - y = -4$
  $x + 2y = 5$

EXAMPLE 2 **Solve by Linear Combinations**

Solve the linear system. $2x + 4y = 10$ Equation 1

  $3y = 12 - 2x$ Equation 2

SOLUTION

Arrange the equations with like terms in columns.

  $2x + 4y = 10$ Write Equation 1.

  $2x + 3y = 12$ Rearrange Equation 2.

Multiply Equation 2 by -1 to get the coefficients of x to be opposites.

  $2x + 4y = 10$ $2x + 4y = 10$

  $2x + 3y = 12$ Multiply by -1. $-2x - 3y = -12$

           Add the equations. $y = -2$

Substitute -2 for y into either equation and solve for x.

  $2x + 4y = 10$ Write Equation 1.

  $2x + 4(-2) = 10$ Substitute -2 for y.

  $2x - 8 = 10$ Multiply.

  $2x = 18$ Add 8 to both sides.

  $x = 9$ Solve for x.

The solution is $(9, -2)$.

(continued)

Practice with Examples

For use with pages 402–408

Check the solution in each of the original equations.

First check the solution in Equation 1.

$$2x + 4y = 10 \qquad \text{Write Equation 1.}$$
$$2(9) + 4(-2) \stackrel{?}{=} 10 \qquad \text{Substitute 9 for } x \text{ and } -2 \text{ for } y.$$
$$18 - 8 \stackrel{?}{=} 10 \qquad \text{Multiply.}$$
$$10 = 10 \qquad \text{Subtract.}$$

Then check the solution in Equation 2.

$$2x + 3y = 12 \qquad \text{Write Equation 2.}$$
$$2(9) + 3(-2) \stackrel{?}{=} 12 \qquad \text{Substitute 9 for } x \text{ and } -2 \text{ for } y.$$
$$18 - 6 \stackrel{?}{=} 12 \qquad \text{Multiply.}$$
$$12 = 12 \qquad \text{Subtract.}$$

Exercises for Example 2

Solve the linear systems. Then check your solutions.

7. $3x + 4y = 12$
$2x + 4y = 10$

8. $6x + 5y = 10$
$6x - 2y = 3$

9. $-4x - 3y = 8$
$-4x + 2y = -2$

Algebra 1, Concepts and Skills
Practice Workbook with Examples

NAME _____ DATE _____

Practice with Examples

For use with pages 409–414

GOAL Use linear systems to solve real-life problems.

EXAMPLE 1 *Choosing a Solution Method*

Your cousin borrowed $6000, some on a home-equity loan at an interest rate of 9.5% and the rest on a consumer loan at an interest rate of 11%. Her total interest paid was $645. How much did she borrow at each rate?

SOLUTION

Verbal Model

| Home-equity loan amount | + | Consumer loan amount | = | Total loan |

| Home-equity loan rate | · | Home-equity loan amount | + | Consumer loan rate | · | Consumer loan amount | = |

| Total interest paid |

Labels

Home-equity loan amount = x	(dollars)
Consumer loan amount =, y	(dollars)
Total loan = 6000	(dollars)
Home-equity loan rate = 0.095	(percent written in decimal form)
Consumer loan rate = 0.11	(percent written in decimal form)
Total interest paid = 645	(dollars)

Algebraic Model

$x + y = 6000$ Equation 1 (loan)
$0.095x + 0.11y = 645$ Equation 2 (interest)

Because the coefficients of x and y are 1 in Equation 1, use the substitution method. You can solve Equation 1 for x and substitute the result into Equation 2. You will obtain 5000 for y. Substitute 5000 into Equation 1 and solve for x. You will obtain 1000 for x.

The solution is $1000 borrowed at 9.5% and $5000 borrowed at 11%.

NAME _____ DATE _____

Practice with Examples

For use with pages 409–414

Exercise for Example 1

1. Choose a method to solve the linear system. Explain your choice.

a. $2x - y = 3$

  $x + 3y = 5$

b. $4x + 4y = 16$

  $-2x + 5y = 9$

c. $x - 3y = 3$

  $5x + 2y = 14$

EXAMPLE 2 *Solving a Cost Problem*

For a community bake sale, you purchased 12 pounds of sugar and 15 pounds of flour. Your total cost was $9.30. The next day, at the same prices, you purchased 4 pounds of sugar and 10 pounds of flour. Your total cost the second day was $4.60. Find the cost per pound of the sugar and the flour purchases.

SOLUTION

Verbal Model	Amount of sugar Day 1	$\cdot$	Cost of sugar	$+$	Amount of flour Day 1	$\cdot$	Cost of flour	$=$	Total cost Day 1
	Amount of sugar Day 2	$\cdot$	Cost of sugar	$+$	Amount of flour Day 2	$\cdot$	Cost of flour	$=$	Total cost Day 2

(continued)

LESSON
7.4
CONTINUED

NAME _____ DATE _____

Practice with Examples

For use with pages 409–414

Labels	Amount of sugar Day 1 = 12	(pounds)
	Amount of flour Day 1 = 15	(pounds)
	Amount of sugar Day 2 = 4	(pounds)
	Amount of flour Day 2 = 10	(pounds)
	Cost of sugar = x	(dollars per pound)
	Cost of flour = y	(dollars per pound)
	Total cost Day 1 = 9.30	(dollars)
	Total cost Day 2 = 4.60	(dollars)

Algebraic $12x + 15y = 9.30$ Equation 1 (Purchases–Day 1)
Model $4x + 10y = 4.60$ Equation 2 (Purchases–Day 2)

Use linear combinations to solve this linear system because none of the variables has a coefficient of 1 or −1. You can get the coefficients of x to be opposites by multiplying Equation 2 by −3. You will obtain 0.30 for y. Substitute 0.30 for y into Equation 1 and solve for x. You will obtain 0.40 for x.

The solution of the linear system is (0.40, 0.30). You conclude that sugar costs $.40 per pound and flour costs $.30 per pound.

Exercise for Example 2

2. Rework Example 2 if the cost of the first purchase was $7.95 and the cost of the second purchase was $3.90.

NAME _____ DATE _____

Practice with Examples

For use with pages 415–422

GOAL **Identify how many solutions a linear system has**

EXAMPLE 1 *A Linear System with No Solution*

Show that the linear system has no solution.

$3x - y = 1$ Equation 1

$3x - y = -2$ Equation 2

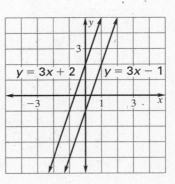

$y = 3x + 2$ $y = 3x - 1$

SOLUTION

Method 1:   GRAPHING Rewrite each equation in slope-intercept form. Then graph the linear system.

$y = 3x - 1$ Revised Equation 1

$y = 3x + 2$ Revised Equation 2

Because the lines have the same slope but different y-intercepts, they are parallel. Parallel lines never intersect, so the system has no solution.

Method 2:   SUBSTITUTION Because Equation 2 can be revised to $y = 3x + 2$, you can substitute $3x + 2$ for y in Equation 1.

$3x - y = 1$ Write Equation 1.

$3x - (3x + 2) \stackrel{?}{=} 1$ Substitute $3x + 2$ for y.

$-2 \neq 1$ Simplify. False statement.

The variables are eliminated and you have a statement that is not true regardless of the values of x and y. The system has no solution.

Exercises for Example 1

Use the substitution method or linear combinations to solve the linear system and tell how many solutions the system has.

1. $2x - y = 1$
     $6x - 3y = 12$

2. $x + y = 5$
     $3x + 3y = 7$

3. $2x + 6y = 6$
     $x + 3y = -3$

Algebra 1, Concepts and Skills
Practice Workbook with Examples

Practice with Examples

For use with pages 415–422

EXAMPLE 2 *A Linear System with Infinitely Many Solutions*

Use linear combinations to show that the linear system has infinitely many solutions.

$$3x + y = 4 \qquad \text{Equation 1}$$
$$6x + 2y = 8 \qquad \text{Equation 2}$$

SOLUTION

You can multiply Equation 1 by -2.

$$-6x - 2y = -8 \qquad \text{Multiply Equation 1 by } -2.$$
$$\underline{6x + 2y = 8} \qquad \text{Write Equation 2.}$$
$$0 = 0 \qquad \text{Add the equations.}$$

The variables are eliminated and you have a statement that is true regardless of the values of x and y. The system has infinitely many solutions.

Exercises for Example 2

Use linear combinations to solve the linear system and tell how many solutions the system has.

4. $2x + 3y = 6$
   $6x + 9y = 18$

5. $4x + 6y = 12$
   $6x + 9y = 18$

6. $4x - 2y = 6$
   $2x - y = 3$

Practice with Examples

For use with pages 415–422

EXAMPLE 3 *Identifying the Number of Solutions*

Solve the linear system and tell how many solutions the system has.

a. $2x + 3y = 10$
$6x + 9y = 30$

b. $\quad 3x - 8y = 21$
$-15x + 40y = 105$

SOLUTION

a. Use linear combinations.

You can multiply Equation 1 by 3 to obtain Equation 2.

$\qquad 6x + 9y = 30$ Revised Equation 1

$\qquad 6x + 9y = 30$ Equation 2

The equations are identical. The linear system has infinitely many solutions.

b. Use linear combinations.

$\qquad 3x - 8y = 21$ Multiply Equation 1 by 5. $15x - 40y = 105$

$-15x + 40y = 105$ $\underline{-15x + 40y = 105}$

                       Add equations. $0 \neq 210$

The resulting statement is false. The linear system has no solutions.

Exercises for Example 3

Solve the linear system and tell how many solutions the system has.

7. $9x + 6y = 24$
$\quad -2x - 5y = -20$

8. $-2x + 8y = 14$
$\quad 6x - 24y = 30$

NAME _____ DATE _____

Practice with Examples

For use with pages 423–430

GOAL Graph a system of linear inequalities.

VOCABULARY

Two or more linear inequalities in the same variables form a **system of linear inequalities** or simply a **system of inequalities.**

A **solution of a system of linear inequalities** in two variables is an ordered pair that is a solution of each inequality in the system.

EXAMPLE 1 *Graph a System of Inequalities*

Graph the system of linear inequalities.

$x - y \geq 0$ Inequality 1

$x + y \geq 0$ Inequality 2

$x \leq 3$ Inequality 3

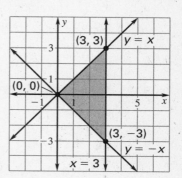

SOLUTION

Graph all three inequalities in the same coordinate plane. The graph of the system is the overlap, or intersection, of the three half-planes shown.

Exercises for Example 1

Graph the system of linear inequalities.

1. $x + y \leq 5$
   $x > 1$
   $y > -1$

2. $2x + 3y < 6$
   $2x + y \leq 2$

3. $y \geq x - 1$
   $y \leq -x + 1$
   $y \geq -1$

Algebra 1, Concepts and Skills
Practice Workbook with Examples

NAME _____ DATE _____

Practice with Examples

For use with pages 423–430

EXAMPLE 2 *Write a System of Linear Inequalities*

Write a system of linear inequalities that
defines the shaded region shown.

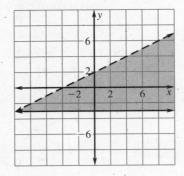

SOLUTION

Since the shaded region is bounded by two lines,
you know that the system must have two linear
inequalities.

Inequality 1 The first inequality is bounded by
the line that passes through the points (0, 2) and
(6, 5). The slope of this line can be found using
the formula for slope.

$$m = \frac{y_2 - y_1}{x_2 - x_1} \qquad \text{Write formula for slope.}$$

$$m = \frac{5 - 2}{6 - 0} \qquad \text{Substitute coordinates into formula.}$$

$$m = \frac{3}{6} = \frac{1}{2} \qquad \text{Simplify.}$$

Since (0, 2) is the point where the line crosses the *y*-axis, an equation for
this line can be found using the slope-intercept form.

$$y = mx + b \qquad \text{Write slope-intercept form.}$$

$$y = \frac{1}{2}x + 2 \qquad \text{Substitute } \frac{1}{2} \text{ for } m \text{ and 2 for } b.$$

Since the shaded region is *below* this *dashed* boundary line, the inequality
is $y < \frac{1}{2}x + 2$.

Inequality 2 The second inequality is bounded by the horizontal line that
passes through the point (0, −3). An equation of this line is $y = -3$.
Since the shaded region is above this solid boundary line, the inequality
is $y \geq -3$.

The system of inequalities that defines the shaded region is:

$$y < \frac{1}{2}x + 2$$

$$y \geq -3$$

Practice with Examples

For use with pages 423–430

Exercises for Example 2

Write a system of linear inequalities that defines the shaded region.

4.

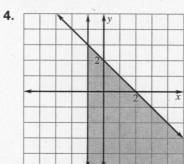

NAME _____ DATE _____

Practice with Examples

For use with pages 441–448

GOAL **Use multiplication properties of exponents.**

VOCABULARY

Let a and b be real numbers and let m and n be positive integers.

Product of Powers Property
To multiply powers having the same base, add the exponents.
$a^m \cdot a^n = a^{m+n}$ Example: $3^2 \cdot 3^7 = 3^{2+7} = 3^9$

Power of a Power Property
To find a power of a power, multiply the exponents.
$(a^m)^n = a^{m \cdot n}$ Example: $(5^2)^4 = 5^{2 \cdot 4} = 5^8$

Power of a Product Property
To find a power of a product, find the power of each factor and multiply.
$(a \cdot b)^m = a^m \cdot b^m$ Example: $(2 \cdot 3)^6 = 2^6 \cdot 3^6$

EXAMPLE 1 *Using the Product of Powers Property*

a. $4^3 \cdot 4^5$ **b.** $(-x)(-x)^2$

SOLUTION

To multiply powers having the same base, add the exponents.

a. $4^3 \cdot 4^5 = 4^{3+5}$ **b.** $(-x)(-x)^2 = (-x)^1(-x)^2$
$\qquad\qquad\ = 4^8$ $= (-x)^{1+2}$
$\qquad\qquad\qquad\qquad\qquad\qquad\qquad\qquad\qquad\quad = (-x)^3$

Exercises for Example 1

Use the product of powers property to simplify the expression.

1. $m \cdot m$

2. $6^2 \cdot 6^3$

3. $y^4 \cdot y^3$

4. $3 \cdot 3^5$

NAME _____ DATE _____

Practice with Examples

For use with pages 441–448

EXAMPLE 2 *Using the Power of a Power Property*

---

a. $(z^4)^5$

b. $(2^3)^2$

SOLUTION

To find a power of a power, multiply the exponents.

a. $(z^4)^5 = z^{4 \cdot 5}$

$= z^{20}$

b. $(2^3)^2 = 2^{3 \cdot 2}$

$= 2^6$

Exercises for Example 2

Use the power of a power property to simplify the expression.

5. $(w^7)^3$

6. $(7^3)^5$

7. $(t^2)^6$

8. $[(-2)^3]^2$

EXAMPLE 3 *Using the Power of a Product Property*

Simplify $(-4mn)^2$.

SOLUTION

To find a power of a product, find the power of each factor and multiply.

$(-4mn)^2 = (-4 \cdot m \cdot n)^2$ Identify factors.

$= (-4)^2 \cdot m^2 \cdot n^2$ Raise each factor to a power.

$= 16m^2n^2$ Simplify.

Practice with Examples

For use with pages 441–448

Exercises for Example 3

Use the power of a product property to simplify the expression.

9. $(5x)^3$

10. $(10s)^2$

11. $(-x)^4$

12. $(-3y)^3$

EXAMPLE 4 *Using Powers to Model Real-Life Problems*

You are planting two square vegetable gardens. The side of the larger garden is twice as long as the side of the smaller garden. Find the ratio of the area of the larger garden to the area of the smaller garden.

SOLUTION

$$\text{Ratio} = \frac{(2x)^2}{x^2} = \frac{2^2 \cdot x^2}{x^2} = \frac{4x^2}{x^2} = \frac{4}{1}$$

Exercise for Example 4

13. Rework Example 4 if the side of the larger garden is three times as long as the side of the smaller garden.

Algebra 1, Concepts and Skills
Practice Workbook with Examples

Practice with Examples

For use with pages 449–454

GOAL Evaluate powers that have zero or negative exponents.

VOCABULARY

Let a be a nonzero number and let n be an integer.

- A nonzero number to the zero power is 1: $a^0 = 1,\ a \neq 0$.

- a^{-n} is the reciprocal of a^n: $a^{-n} = \dfrac{1}{a^n},\ a \neq 0$.

EXAMPLE 1 *Powers with Zero and Negative Exponents*

Evaluate the exponential expression.

a. $(-8)^0$ b. 4^{-2}

SOLUTION

a. $(-8)^0 = 1$ A nonzero number to the zero power is 1.

b. $4^{-2} = \dfrac{1}{4^2} = \dfrac{1}{16}$ 4^{-2} is the reciprocal of 4^2.

Exercises for Example 1

Evaluate the exponential expression.

1. 73^0

2. $\left(\frac{1}{2}\right)^{-1}$

3. 13^{-2}

Practice with Examples

For use with pages 449–454

EXAMPLE 2 *Simplifying Exponential Expressions*

Rewrite the expression with positive exponents.

a. $5y^{-1}z^{-2}$ **b.** $(2x)^{-3}$

SOLUTION

a. $5y^{-1}z^{-2} = 5 \cdot \dfrac{1}{y} \cdot \dfrac{1}{z^2} = \dfrac{5}{yz^2}$

b. $(2x)^{-3} = 2^{-3} \cdot x^{-3}$ Use power of a product property.

$\quad = \dfrac{1}{2^3} \cdot \dfrac{1}{x^3}$ Write reciprocals of 2^3 and x^3.

$\quad = \dfrac{1}{8x^3}$ Multiply fractions.

Exercises for Example 2

Rewrite the expression with positive exponents.

4. $(13y)^{-1}$

5. $\dfrac{1}{(2x)^{-4}}$

6. $(2c)^{-4}d$

Algebra 1, Concepts and Skills
Practice Workbook with Examples

Practice with Examples

For use with pages 449–454

EXAMPLE 3 *Evaluating Exponential Expressions*

Evaluate the expression.

a. $(3^{-2})^{-3}$　　　　　**b.** $2^{-2} \cdot 2^{-1}$

SOLUTION

a. $(3^{-2})^{-3} = 3^{-2 \cdot (-3)}$　　Use power of a power property.

$\qquad\qquad = 3^6$　　　　　Multiply exponents.

$\qquad\qquad = 729$　　　　　Evaluate.

b. $2^{-2} \cdot 2^{-1} = 2^{-2 + (-1)}$　　Use product of powers property.

$\qquad\qquad = 2^{-3}$　　　　　Add exponents.

$\qquad\qquad = \dfrac{1}{2^3}$　　　　2^{-3} is the reciprocal of 2^3.

$\qquad\qquad = \dfrac{1}{8}$　　　　　Evaluate power.

Exercises for Example 3

Evaluate the expression.

7. $8^{-1} \cdot 8^1$

8. $4^6 \cdot 4^{-4}$

9. $(5^{-2})^2$

NAME _____ DATE _____

Practice with Examples

For use with pages 455–461

GOAL **Graph an exponential function.**

VOCABULARY

A function of the form $y = a \cdot b^x$, where $b > 0$ and $b \neq 1$ is an **exponential function.**

EXAMPLE 1 *Evaluate and Graph an Exponential Function When b > 1*

a. Make a table of values for the exponential function $y = 5^x$. Use x-values of $-2, -1, 0, 1,$ and 2.

b. Use the table of values to graph the function $y = 5^x$.

SOLUTION

a.

x	-2	-1	0	1	2
$y = 5^x$	$\frac{1}{25}$	$\frac{1}{5}$	1	5	25

b.

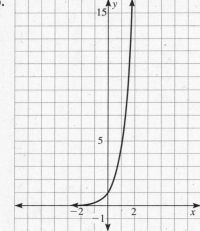

Exercise for Example 1

1. Evaluate and graph the exponential function $y = 4^x$. Use x-values of $-2, -1, 0, 1,$ and 2.

Practice with Examples

For use with pages 455–461

EXAMPLE 2 *Evaluate and Graph an Exponential Function When 0 < b < 1*

a. Make a table of values for the exponential function $y = \left(\frac{1}{3}\right)^x$. Use x-values of $-2, -1, 0, 1,$ and 2.

b. Use the table of values to graph the function $y = \left(\frac{1}{3}\right)^x$.

SOLUTION

a.

x	-2	-1	0	1	2
$y = \left(\frac{1}{3}\right)^x$	9	3	1	$\frac{1}{3}$	$\frac{1}{9}$

b.

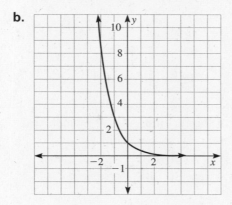

Exercise for Example 2

2. Evaluate and graph the exponential function $y = 2\left(\frac{1}{2}\right)^x$. Use the x-values $-2, -1, 0, 1,$ and 2.

NAME _____ DATE _____

Practice with Examples

For use with pages 455–461

EXAMPLE 3 *Find Domain and Range*

a. Describe the domain and range of the function $y = 5^x$, which is graphed in Example 1.

b. Describe the domain and range of the function $y = \left(\dfrac{1}{3}\right)^x$, which is graphed in Example 2.

SOLUTION

a. The domain of $y = 5^x$ is all real numbers; the range of $y = 5^x$ is all positive real numbers.

b. The domain of $y = \left(\dfrac{1}{3}\right)^x$ is all real numbers; the range of $y = \left(\dfrac{1}{3}\right)^x$ is all positive real numbers.

Exercises for Example 3

3. Describe the domain and range of the function $y = 4^x$, which you graphed in Exercise 1.

4. Describe the domain and range of the function $y = 2\left(\dfrac{1}{2}\right)^x$, which you graphed in Exercise 2.

Algebra 1, Concepts and Skills
Practice Workbook with Examples

NAME _____ DATE _____

Practice with Examples

For use with pages 462–468

GOAL **Use division properties of exponents.**

VOCABULARY

Let a and b be real numbers and let m and n be integers.

Quotient of Powers Property

To divide powers having the same base, subtract exponents.

$$\frac{a^m}{a^n} = a^{m-n}, \ a \neq 0 \qquad \text{Example: } \frac{3^7}{3^5} = 3^{7-5} = 3^2$$

Power of a Quotient Property

To find a power of a quotient, find the power of the numerator and the power of the denominator and divide.

$$\left(\frac{a}{b}\right)^m = \frac{a^m}{b^m}, \ b \neq 0 \qquad \text{Example: } \left(\frac{4}{5}\right)^3 = \frac{4^3}{5^3}$$

EXAMPLE 1 *Using the Quotient of Powers Property*

Use the quotient of powers property to simplify the expression.

a. $\dfrac{8^2 \cdot 8^4}{8^3}$

b. $z^7 \cdot \dfrac{1}{z^8}$

SOLUTION

To divide powers having the same base, subtract exponents.

a. $\dfrac{8^2 \cdot 8^4}{8^3} = \dfrac{8^6}{8^3}$

$= 8^{6-3}$

$= 8^3$

b. $z^7 \cdot \dfrac{1}{z^8} = \dfrac{z^7}{z^8}$

$= z^{7-8}$

$= z^{-1}$

$= \dfrac{1}{z}$

Exercises for Example 1

Use the quotient of powers property to simplify the expression.

1. $\dfrac{10^4}{10}$

2. $\dfrac{3^2}{3^3}$

3. $\dfrac{1}{y^2} \cdot y^8$

Algebra 1, Concepts and Skills
Practice Workbook with Examples

Practice with Examples

For use with pages 462–468

EXAMPLE 2 *Simplifying an Expression*

Simplify the expression $\left(\dfrac{7a}{b^2}\right)^3$.

SOLUTION

$$\left(\frac{7a}{b^2}\right)^3 = \frac{(7a)^3}{(b^2)^3} \qquad \text{Power of a quotient}$$

$$= \frac{7^3 \cdot a^3}{b^6} \qquad \text{Power of a product and power of a power}$$

$$= \frac{343a^3}{b^6} \qquad \text{Simplify.}$$

Exercises for Example 2

Simplify the expression.

4. $\left(\dfrac{2}{x^3}\right)^4$

5. $\dfrac{z \cdot z^5}{z^2}$

6. $\left(\dfrac{5y^2}{w}\right)^2$

Algebra 1, Concepts and Skills
Practice Workbook with Examples

Practice with Examples

For use with pages 462–468

EXAMPLE 3 *Simplifying Expressions with Negative Exponents*

Simplify the expression $\left(\dfrac{6x^2y^{-1}}{2xy^3}\right)^{-2}$. Use only positive exponents.

SOLUTION

$$\left(\frac{6x^2y^{-1}}{2xy^3}\right)^{-2} = \frac{(6x^2y^{-1})^{-2}}{(2xy^3)^{-2}} \qquad \text{Power of a quotient}$$

$$= \frac{(2xy^3)^2}{(6x^2y^{-1})^2} \qquad \text{Definition of negative exponents}$$

$$= \frac{4x^2y^6}{36x^4y^{-2}} \qquad \text{Power of a product and power of a power}$$

$$= \frac{x^{-2}y^8}{9} \qquad \text{Quotient of powers}$$

$$= \frac{y^8}{9x^2} \qquad \text{Definition of negative exponents}$$

Exercises for Example 3

Simplify the expression. Use only positive exponents.

7. $\dfrac{5x^2y^{-3}}{2x^4}$

8. $\left(\dfrac{3x^{-4}y^5}{xy^{-2}}\right)^{-1}$

9. $\left(\dfrac{x^3}{y^{-2}}\right)^{-2} \cdot \dfrac{y^4x^2}{x^{-1}}$

NAME _____ DATE _____

Practice with Examples

For use with pages 469–474

GOAL **Read and write numbers in scientific notation.**

VOCABULARY

A number is written in **scientific notation** if it is of the form $c \times 10^n$, where $1 \dagger c < 10$ and n is an integer.

EXAMPLE 1 *Rewriting in Decimal Form*

Rewrite each number in decimal form.

a. 2.23×10^4 **b.** 8.5×10^{-3}

SOLUTION

a. $2.23 \times 10^4 = 22{,}300$ Move decimal point to the right 4 places.

b. $8.5 \times 10^{-3} = 0.0085$ Move decimal point to the left 3 places.

Exercises for Example 1

Rewrite each number in decimal form.

1. 9.332×10^6

2. 2.78×10^{-1}

3. 4.5×10^5

EXAMPLE 2 *Rewriting in Scientific Notation*

Rewrite each number in scientific notation.

a. 0.0729 **b.** $26{,}645$

SOLUTION

a. $0.0729 = 7.29 \times 10^{-2}$ Move decimal point to the right 2 places.

b. $26{,}645 = 2.6645 \times 10^4$ Move decimal point to the left 4 places.

Practice with Examples

For use with pages 469–474

Exercises for Example 2

Rewrite each number in scientific notation.

4. 75.2

5. 135,667

6. 0.00088

EXAMPLE 3 *Computing with Scientific Notation*

Evaluate the expression and write the result in scientific notation.

$(7.0 \times 10^4)^2$

SOLUTION

To multiply, divide, or find powers of numbers in scientific notation, use the properties of exponents.

$(7.0 \times 10^4)^2 = 7.0^2 \times (10^4)^2$ Power of a product

$= 49 \times 10^8$ Power of a power

$= 4.9 \times 10^9$ Write in scientific notation.

Exercises for Example 3

Evaluate the expression and write the result in scientific notation.

7. $(2.3 \times 10^{-1})(5.5 \times 10^3)$

8. $(2.0 \times 10^{-1})^3$

Algebra 1, Concepts and Skills
Practice Workbook with Examples

Practice with Examples

For use with pages 469–474

EXAMPLE 4 *Dividing with Scientific Notation*

The mass of the sun is approximately 1.99×10^{30} kilograms. The mass of the moon is approximately 7.36×10^{22} kilograms. The mass of the sun is approximately how many times that of the moon?

SOLUTION

Find the ratio of the mass of the sun to the mass of the moon.

$$\frac{1.99 \times 10^{30}}{7.36 \times 10^{22}} \approx 0.27 \times 10^{8}$$

$$\approx 2.7 \times 10^{7}$$

The mass of the sun is about 27,000,000 times that of the moon.

Exercise for Example 4

9. The Pacific Ocean covers about 1.66241×10^{8} square kilometers. The Baltic Sea covers about 4.144×10^{5} square kilometers. The Pacific Ocean is approximately how many times as large as the Baltic Sea?

NAME _____ DATE _____

Practice with Examples

For use with pages 475–481

GOAL **Write and use models for exponential growth and graph models for exponential growth**

VOCABULARY

Exponential growth occurs when a quantity increases by the same percent r in each time period t.

C is the initial amount. ⟶   ⌐ t is the time period.

$$y = C(1 + r)^t$$

The percent of increase is $100r$. $(1 + r)$ is the growth factor, r is the growth rate.

EXAMPLE 1 *Finding the Balance in an Account*

A principal of $600 is deposited in an account that pays 3.5% interest compounded yearly. Find the account balance after 4 years.

SOLUTION

Use the exponential growth model to find the account balance A.
The growth rate is 0.035. The initial value is 600.

$A = P(1 + r)^t$	Exponential growth model
$= 600(1 + 0.035)^4$	Substitute 600 for P, 0.035 for r, and 4 for t.
$= 600(1.035)^4$	Simplify.
≈ 688.514	Evaluate.

The balance after 4 years will be about $688.51.

Exercises for Example 1

Use the exponential growth model to find the account balance.

1. A principal of $450 is deposited in an account that pays 2.5% interest compounded yearly. Find the account balance after 2 years.

2. A principal of $800 is deposited in an account that pays 3% interest compounded yearly. Find the account balance after 5 years.

Practice with Examples

For use with pages 475–481

EXAMPLE 2 *Writing an Exponential Growth Model*

A population of 40 pheasants is released in a wildlife preserve. The population doubles each year for 3 years. What is the population after 4 years?

SOLUTION

Because the population doubles each year, the growth factor is 2. Then $1 + r = 2$, and the growth rate $r = 1$.

$$
\begin{aligned}
P &= C(1 + r)^t && \text{Exponential growth model} \\
&= 40(1 + 1)^4 && \text{Substitute for } C, r, \text{ and } t. \\
&= 40 \cdot 2^4 && \text{Simplify.} \\
&= 640 && \text{Evaluate.}
\end{aligned}
$$

After 4 years, the population will be about 640 pheasants.

Exercise for Example 2

3. A population of 50 pheasants is released in a wildlife preserve. The population triples each year for 3 years. What is the population after 3 years?

Practice with Examples

For use with pages 475–481

EXAMPLE 3 *Graphing an Exponential Growth Model*

Graph the exponential growth model in Example 2.

SOLUTION

Make a table of values, plot the points in a coordinate plane, and draw a smooth curve through the points.

t	0	1	2	3	4	5
P	40	80	160	320	640	1280

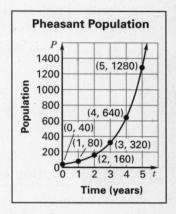

Pheasant Population

Exercise for Example 3

4. Graph the exponential growth model in Exercise 3.

Practice with Examples

For use with pages 482–488

GOAL **Write and graph exponential decay functions.**

VOCABULARY

Exponential decay occurs when a quantity decreases by the same percent r in each time period t.

C is the initial amount. ──────┐   ┌── t is the time period.

$$y = C(1 - r)^t$$

The percent of decrease is $100r$. $(1 - r)$ is the decay factor, r is the decay rate.

EXAMPLE 1 **Writing an Exponential Decay Model**

You bought a used truck for $15,000. The value of the truck will decrease each year because of depreciation. The truck depreciates at the rate of 8% per year. Write an exponential decay model to represent the real-life problem.

SOLUTION

The initial value C is $15,000. The decay rate r is 0.08. Let y be the value and let t be the age of the truck in years.

$y = C(1 - r)^t$	Exponential decay model
$\quad = 15,000(1 - 0.08)^t$	Substitute 15,000 for C and 0.08 for r.
$\quad = 15,000(0.92)^t$	Simplify.

The exponential decay model is $y = 15,000(0.92)^t$.

Exercises for Example 1

1. Use the exponential decay model in Example 1 to estimate the value of your truck in 5 years.

Practice with Examples

For use with pages 482–488

2. Use the exponential decay model in Example 1 to estimate the value of your truck in 7 years.

3. Rework Example 1 if the truck depreciates at the rate of 10% per year.

Practice with Examples

For use with pages 482–488

EXAMPLE 2 *Graphing an Exponential Decay Model*

a. Graph the exponential decay model in Example 1.

b. Use the graph to estimate the value of your truck in 6 years.

SOLUTION

a. Make a table of values for the model in Example 1.

Year	Value
0	15,000
1	$15{,}000(0.92) = 13{,}800$
2	$15{,}000(0.92)^2 = 12{,}696$
3	$15{,}000(0.92)^3 \approx 11{,}680$
4	$15{,}000(0.92)^4 \approx 10{,}746$
5	$15{,}000(0.92)^5 \approx 9886$

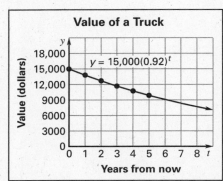

Value of a Truck

Use the table of values to write ordered pairs:
(0, 15,000), (1, 13,800), (2, 12,696), (3, 11,680),
(4, 10,746), (5, 9886). Plot the points in a
coordinate plane, and draw a smooth curve
through the points.

b. From the graph, the value of your truck in 6 years is about $9100.

Exercises for Example 2

4. Use the graph in Example 2 to estimate the value of your truck
in 8 years.

5. Graph the exponential decay model in Exercise 3.

Algebra 1, Concepts and Skills
Practice Workbook with Examples

Practice with Examples

For use with pages 499–504

GOAL Evaluate and approximate square roots

VOCABULARY

If $b^2 = a$, then b is a **square root** of a.

A square root b can be a **positive square root** (or a principal square root) or a **negative square root**.

A **radicand** is the number or expression inside a radical symbol $\sqrt{\ }$.

Perfect squares are numbers whose square roots are integers.

A number that is not the quotient of integers is an **irrational number**.

A **radical expression** is an expression written with a radical symbol.

EXAMPLE 1 *Finding Square Roots of Numbers*

Evaluate the expression.

a. $\sqrt{81}$

b. $-\sqrt{49}$

c. $\pm\sqrt{16}$

d. $\sqrt{0}$

SOLUTION

a. $\sqrt{81} = 9$ Positive square root

b. $-\sqrt{49} = -7$ Negative square root

c. $\pm\sqrt{16} = \pm 4$ Two square roots

d. $\sqrt{0} = 0$ Square root of zero is zero.

Practice with Examples

For use with pages 499–504

Exercises for Example 1

Evaluate the expression.

1. $\sqrt{9}$

2. $\sqrt{36}$

3. $-\sqrt{25}$

4. $\pm\sqrt{100}$

EXAMPLE 2 *Evaluating a Radical Expression*

Evaluate $\sqrt{b^2 - 4ac}$ when $a = -2$, $b = -5$, and $c = 2$.

SOLUTION

$$\sqrt{b^2 - 4ac} = \sqrt{(-5)^2 - 4(-2)(2)} \quad \text{Substitute values.}$$

$$= \sqrt{25 + 16} \quad \text{Simplify.}$$

$$= \sqrt{41} \quad \text{Simplify.}$$

$$\approx 6.40 \quad \text{Round to the nearest hundredth.}$$

Algebra 1, Concepts and Skills
Practice Workbook with Examples

Practice with Examples

For use with pages 499–504

Exercises for Example 2

Evaluate $\sqrt{b^2 - 4ac}$ for the given values.

5. $a = -3, b = 6, c = -3$

6. $a = 1, b = 5, c = 4$

Algebra 1, Concepts and Skills
Practice Workbook with Examples

NAME _____ DATE _____

Practice with Examples

For use with pages 505–510

GOAL Solve a quadratic equation by finding square roots

> **VOCABULARY**
>
> A **quadratic equation** is an equation that can be written in the standard form $ax^2 + bx + c = 0$, where $a \neq 0$. In standard form, a is the *leading coefficient*.

EXAMPLE 1 *Solving Quadratic Equations*

Solve $x^2 = 19$.

SOLUTION

$x^2 = 19$ Write original equation.

$x = \pm \sqrt{19}$ Find square roots.

Since 19 is not a perfect square, the solutions are $\sqrt{19}$ and $-\sqrt{19}$.

Exercises for Example 1

Solve the equation or write *no real solution*. Write the solutions as integers if possible. Otherwise, write them as radical expressions.

  1. $x^2 = 36$

  2. $x^2 = 15$

  3. $y^2 = 25$

Practice with Examples

For use with pages 505–510

EXAMPLE 2 *Rewriting Before Finding Square Roots*

Solve $4x^2 - 100 = 0$.

SOLUTION

$4x^2 - 100 = 0$	Write original equation.
$4x^2 = 100$	Add 100 to each side.
$x^2 = 25$	Divide each side by 4.
$x = \pm\sqrt{25}$	Find square roots.
$x = \pm 5$	25 is a perfect square.

Exercises for Example 2

Solve the equation or write *no real solution*. Write the solutions as integers if possible. Otherwise, write them as radical expressions.

4. $6x^2 - 54 = 0$

5. $5x^2 - 15 = 0$

6. $2x^2 - 98 = 0$

Algebra 1, Concepts and Skills
Practice Workbook with Examples

Practice with Examples

For use with pages 505–510

EXAMPLE 3 *Writing and Using a Falling Object Model*

A diver jumps from a 80-foot cliff to a lake below. Write a model for the diver's height. (Disregard air resistance.) Then find the time it would take for the diver to reach the water.

SOLUTION

The initial height is $s = 80$ feet.

$h = -16t^2 + s$ Write falling object model.

$h = -16t^2 + 80$ Substitute 80 for s.

The model is $h = -16t^2 + 80$.

$0 = -16t^2 + 80$ Substitute 0 for h.

$-80 = -16t^2$ Subtract 80 from each side.

$5 = t^2$ Divide each side by -16.

$\sqrt{5} = t$ Find the positive square root. The negative square root doesn't make sense in this problem.

$2.2 \approx t$ Use a calculator to evaluate.

The diver will reach the water in about 2.2 seconds

Exercise for Example 3

7. Rework Example 3 if the diver jumps from a 64-foot cliff.

Algebra 1, Concepts and Skills
Practice Workbook with Examples

NAME _____ DATE _____

Practice with Examples

For use with pages 511–517

GOAL Use properties of radicals to simplify radical expressions.

VOCABULARY

Product Property of Radicals The square root of a product equals the product of the square roots of the factors.

$\sqrt{ab} = \sqrt{a} \cdot \sqrt{b}$ when a and b are nonnegative numbers

Quotient Property of Radicals The square root of a quotient equals the quotient of the square roots of the numerator and denominator.

$\sqrt{\dfrac{a}{b}} = \dfrac{\sqrt{a}}{\sqrt{b}}$ when $a \geq 0$ and $b > 0$

An expression with radicals is in **simplest form** if the following are true:

• No perfect square factors other than 1 are in the radicand.

• No fractions are in the radicand.

• No radicals appear in the denominator.

The process of eliminating a radical from a denominator by multiplying the radical expression by an appropriate value of 1 is called *rationalizing the denominator*.

EXAMPLE 1 *Simplifying with the Product Property*

Simplify the expression $\sqrt{147}$.

SOLUTION

You can use the product property to simplify a radical by removing perfect square factors from the radicand.

$$\sqrt{147} = \sqrt{49 \cdot 3} \qquad \text{Factor using perfect square factor.}$$
$$= \sqrt{49} \cdot \sqrt{3} \qquad \text{Use product property.}$$
$$= 7\sqrt{3} \qquad \text{Simplify.}$$

Exercises for Example 1

Simplify the expression.

1. $\sqrt{98}$ **2.** $\sqrt{52}$

3. $\sqrt{300}$ **4.** $\sqrt{99}$

Practice with Examples
For use with pages 511–517

EXAMPLE 2 *Simplifying with the Quotient Property*

Simplify the expression $\sqrt{\dfrac{27}{48}}$.

SOLUTION

$$\sqrt{\frac{27}{48}} = \frac{\sqrt{3 \cdot 9}}{\sqrt{3 \cdot 16}} \qquad \text{Factor using perfect square factors.}$$

$$= \sqrt{\frac{9}{16}} \qquad \text{Divide out common factors.}$$

$$= \frac{\sqrt{9}}{\sqrt{16}} \qquad \text{Use quotient property.}$$

$$= \frac{3}{4} \qquad \text{Simplify.}$$

Exercises for Example 2

Simplify the expression.

5. $\sqrt{\dfrac{11}{4}}$

6. $\sqrt{\dfrac{1}{100}}$

7. $\sqrt{\dfrac{5}{9}}$

8. $\sqrt{\dfrac{8}{16}}$

Algebra 1, Concepts and Skills
Practice Workbook with Examples

Practice with Examples

For use with pages 511–517

EXAMPLE 3 *Rationalizing the Denominator*

Simplify $\sqrt{\dfrac{5}{2}}$.

SOLUTION

$\sqrt{\dfrac{5}{2}} = \dfrac{\sqrt{5}}{\sqrt{2}}$ Use quotient property.

$= \dfrac{\sqrt{5}}{\sqrt{2}} \cdot \dfrac{\sqrt{2}}{\sqrt{2}}$ Multiply by a value of 1: $\dfrac{\sqrt{2}}{\sqrt{2}} = 1$.

$= \dfrac{\sqrt{10}}{\sqrt{4}}$ Use product property.

$= \dfrac{\sqrt{10}}{2}$ Simplify.

Exercise for Example 3

Simplify the expression.

9. $\sqrt{\dfrac{1}{3}}$

10. $\sqrt{\dfrac{2}{7}}$

11. $\sqrt{\dfrac{27}{15}}$

12. $\sqrt{\dfrac{16}{12}}$

Practice with Examples

For use with pages 518–525

GOAL **Sketch the graph of a quadratic function**

> **VOCABULARY**
>
> A **quadratic function** is a function that can be written in the *standard form* $y = ax^2 + bx + c$, where $a \neq 0$.
>
> Every quadratic function has a U-shaped graph called a **parabola.**
>
> The **vertex** of a parabola is the lowest point of a parabola that opens up and the highest point of a parabola that opens down.
>
> The **axis of symmetry** of a parabola is the vertical line passing through the vertex.

EXAMPLE 1 *Describing the Graph of a Parabola*

Decide whether the graph of the quadratic function opens *up* or *down*.

a. $y = -x^2 + 3x$ **b.** $y = 4x + 2x^2$

SOLUTION

a. Since the value of a is negative in $y = -x^2 + 3x$ the graph opens down.

b. Since the value of a is positive in $y = 4x + 2x^2$ the graph opens up.

Exercises for Example 1

Decide whether the graph of the function opens *up* or *down*.

1. $y = 6x^2$

2. $y = 1 - 3x^2$

3. $y = -5x^2 + x + 7$

Practice with Examples

For use with pages 518–525

EXAMPLE 2 _Graphing a Quadratic Function with a Positive a-value_

Sketch the graph of $y = x^2 - 2x + 1$.

SOLUTION

The vertex has an x-coordinate of $-\dfrac{b}{2a}$. Find the x-coordinate when $a = 1$ and $b = -2$.

$$-\frac{b}{2a} = -\frac{-2}{2(1)} = 1$$

Make a table of values, using x-values to the left and right of $x = 1$.

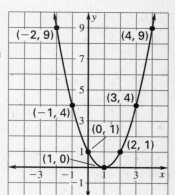

x	-2	-1	0	1	2	3	4
y	9	4	1	0	1	4	9

Plot the points. The vertex is $(1, 0)$ and the axis of symmetry is $x = 1$. Connect the points to form a parabola that opens up because a is positive.

Exercises for Example 2

Sketch the graph of the function. Label the coordinates of the vertex.

4. $y = 2x^2$

5. $y = x^2 + 3x$

6. $y = x^2 + 2x + 1$

NAME _____ DATE _____

Practice with Examples

For use with pages 518–525

EXAMPLE 3 *Graphing a Quadratic Function with a Negative a-value*

Sketch the graph of $y = -x^2 + 2x - 3$.

SOLUTION

The vertex has an x-coordinate of $-\dfrac{b}{2a}$. Find the
x-coordinate when $a = -1$ and $b = 2$.

$$-\frac{b}{2a} = -\frac{2}{2(-1)} = 1$$

Make a table of values, using x-values to the left and right
of $x = 1$.

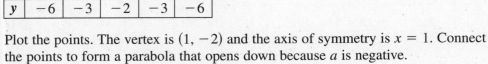

x	-1	0	1	2	3
y	-6	-3	-2	-3	-6

Plot the points. The vertex is $(1, -2)$ and the axis of symmetry is $x = 1$. Connect
the points to form a parabola that opens down because a is negative.

Exercises for Example 3

Sketch the graph of the function. Label the coordinates of the vertex.

7. $y = -4x^2$

8. $y = -x^2 + x$

9. $y = -x^2 - 2x + 3$

NAME _____ DATE _____

Practice with Examples

For use with pages 526–532

GOAL   **Use a graph to find or check a solution of a quadratic equation.**

VOCABULARY

The solutions of a quadratic equation in one variable x can be solved or checked graphically with the following steps.

Step 1: Write the equation in the form $ax^2 + bx + c = 0$.

Step 2: Write the related function $y = ax^2 + bx + c$.

Step 3: Sketch the graph of the function $y = ax^2 + bx + c$.
The solutions, or **roots**, of $ax^2 + bx + c = 0$ are the x-intercepts.

EXAMPLE 1   *Checking a Solution Using a Graph*

_____

a. Solve $3x^2 = 75$ algebraically.   **b.** Check your solution graphically.

SOLUTION

a. $3x^2 = 75$ Write original equation.

    $x^2 = 25$ Divide each side by 3.

     $x = \pm 5$ Find the square root of each side.

b. Write the equation in the form $ax^2 + bx + c = 0$.

     $3x^2 = 75$ Write original equation.

$3x^2 - 75 = 0$ Subtract 75 from each side.

Write the related function $y = ax^2 + bx + c$.

$y = 3x^2 - 75$

Sketch the graph of $y = 3x^2 - 75$. The x-intercepts are ± 5, which agrees with the algebraic solution.

Exercises for Example 1

Solve the equation algebraically. Check the solutions graphically.

1. $\frac{1}{3}x^2 = 12$

2. $3x^2 + 2 = 50$

3. $x^2 - 7 = 2$

Practice with Examples

For use with pages 526–532

EXAMPLE 2 *Solving an Equation by Graphing*

a. Use a graph to estimate the solutions of $x^2 - 3x = 4$.

b. Check your solutions algebraically.

SOLUTION

a. Write the equation in the form
$ax^2 + bx + c = 0$.

$x^2 - 3x = 4$ Write original equation.

$x^2 - 3x - 4 = 0$ Subtract 4 from each side.

Write the related function $y = ax^2 + bx + c$.

$y = x^2 - 3x - 4$

Sketch the graph of the function $y = x^2 - 3x - 4$.

From the graph, the x-intercepts appear to be $x = -1$ and $x = 4$.

b. You can check your solutions algebraically by substitution.

Check $x = -1$:   Check $x = 4$:

$x^2 - 3x = 4$ $x^2 - 3x = 4$

$(-1)^2 - 3(-1) \overset{?}{=} 4$ $4^2 - 3(4) \overset{?}{=} 4$

$1 + 3 = 4$ $16 - 12 = 4$

(graph: parabola $y = x^2 - 3x - 4$ with x-intercepts labeled $(-1, 0)$ and $(4, 0)$, and labels "x-intercepts", "-3", "1", "-5")

Exercises for Example 2

Use a graph to estimate the solutions of the equation. Check the solutions algebraically.

4. $x^2 + x = 12$

5. $x^2 - 5x = -6$

6. $x^2 - 5x = 6$

Algebra 1, Concepts and Skills
Practice Workbook with Examples

NAME _____ DATE _____

Practice with Examples

For use with pages 526–532

EXAMPLE 3 *Points on a Parabola*

The average cost of a license and registration for an automobile in the United States from 1991 through 1997 can be modeled by

$$y = -0.63x^2 + 15.08x + 151.57$$

where y represents the average cost of a license and registration. Let x be the number of years since 1990. Use the graph of the model to estimate the average cost of a license and registration in 1995.

License and Registration Costs

SOLUTION

The year 1995 corresponds to $x = 5$. From the graph of the quadratic equation, the average cost of a license and registration appears to be about 210 dollars.

Exercise for Example 3

7. Check the solution in Example 3 algebraically.

NAME _____ DATE _____

Practice with Examples

For use with pages 533–539

GOAL Use the quadratic formula to solve a quadratic equation.

VOCABULARY

The solutions of the quadratic equation $ax^2 + bx + c = 0$ are given by the **quadratic formula**

$$x = \frac{-b \pm \sqrt{b^2 - 4ac}}{2a} \text{ when } a \neq 0 \text{ and } b^2 - 4ac \neq 0.$$

You can read this formula as "x equals the opposite of b, plus or minus the square root of b squared minus $4ac$, all divided by $2a$."

EXAMPLE 1 *Using the Quadratic Formula*

Solve $x^2 + 3x = 4$.

SOLUTION

You must rewrite the equation in standard form $ax^2 + bx + c = 0$ before using the quadratic formula.

$x^2 + 3x = 4$	Write original equation.
$x^2 + 3x - 4 = 0$	Rewrite equation in standard form.
$1x^2 + 3x + (-4) = 0$	Identify $a = 1$, $b = 3$, and $c = -4$.
$x = \dfrac{-3 \pm \sqrt{3^2 - 4(1)(-4)}}{2(1)}$	Substitute values into the quadratic formula: $a = 1$, $b = 3$, and $c = -4$.
$x = \dfrac{-3 \pm \sqrt{9 + 16}}{2}$	Simplify.
$x = \dfrac{-3 \pm \sqrt{25}}{2}$	Simplify.
$x = \dfrac{-3 \pm 5}{2}$	Solutions

The equation has two solutions:

$$x = \frac{-3 + 5}{2} = 1 \text{ and } x = \frac{-3 - 5}{2} = -4$$

NAME _____ DATE _____

Practice with Examples

For use with pages 533–539

Exercises for Example 1

....

Use the quadratic formula to solve the equation.

1. $x^2 - 4x + 3 = 0$

2. $x^2 + 9x + 20 = 0$

3. $x^2 + x = 6$

Practice with Examples

For use with pages 533–539

EXAMPLE 2 *Modeling Vertical Motion*

You retrieve a football from a tree 25 feet above ground. You throw it downward with an initial speed of 20 feet per second. Use a vertical motion model to find how long it will take for the football to reach the ground.

SOLUTION

Because the football is thrown down, the initial velocity is $v = -20$ feet per second. The initial height is $s = 25$ feet. The football will reach the ground when the height is 0.

$h = -16t^2 + vt + s$	Choose the vertical motion model for a thrown object.
$h = -16t^2 + (-20)t + 25$	Substitute values for v and s into the vertical motion model.
$0 = -16t^2 - 20t + 25$	Substitute 0 for h.
$t = \dfrac{-(-20) \pm \sqrt{(-20)^2 - 4(-16)(25)}}{2(-16)}$	Substitute values into the quadratic formula: $a = -16$, $b = -20$, and $c = 25$.
$t = \dfrac{20 \pm \sqrt{2000}}{-32}$	Simplify.
$t \approx 0.773 \text{ or } -2.022$	Solutions

The football will reach the ground about 0.773 seconds after it was thrown. As a solution, -2.022 doesn't make sense in the problem.

Exercise for Example 2

4. Rework Example 2 if the football is dropped from the tree with an initial speed of 0 feet per second.

Algebra 1, Concepts and Skills
Practice Workbook with Examples

NAME _____ DATE _____

Practice with Examples

For use with pages 540–545

GOAL Use the discriminant to find the number of solutions of a quadratic equation.

VOCABULARY

The **discriminant** is the expression inside the radical in the quadratic formula, $b^2 - 4ac$.

Consider the quadratic equation $ax^2 + bx + c = 0$.

- If $b^2 - 4ac$ is positive, then the equation has two solutions.
- If $b^2 - 4ac$ is zero, then the equation has one solution.
- If $b^2 - 4ac$ is negative, then the equation has no real solution.

EXAMPLE 1 **Finding the Number of Solutions**

Find the value of the discriminant and use the value to tell if the equation has *two solutions, one solution,* or *no real solution.*

a. $3x^2 - 2x - 1 = 0$ **b.** $x^2 - 8x + 16 = 0$ **c.** $x^2 - 4x + 5 = 0$

SOLUTION

a. $b^2 - 4ac = (-2)^2 - 4(3)(-1)$ Substitute 3 for a, -2 for b, -1 for c.

$= 4 + 12$ Simplify.

$= 16$ Discriminant is positive.

The discriminant is positive, so the equation has two solutions.

b. $b^2 - 4ac = (-8)^2 - 4(1)(16)$ Substitute 1 for a, -8 for b, 16 for c.

$= 64 - 64$ Simplify.

$= 0$ Discriminant is zero.

The discriminant is zero, so the equation has one solution.

c. $b^2 - 4ac = (-4)^2 - 4(1)(5)$ Substitute 1 for a, -4 for b, 5 for c.

$= 16 - 20$ Simplify.

$= -4$ Discriminant is negative.

The discriminant is negative, so the equation has no real solution.

NAME _____ DATE _____

Practice with Examples

For use with pages 540–545

Exercises for Example 1

Tell if the equation has *two solutions*, *one solution*, or *no real solution*.

1. $x^2 - 10x + 25 = 0$　　　　　**2.** $2x^2 - x - 1 = 0$

3. $x^2 + 2x + 4 = 0$　　　　　**4.** $-x^2 + 6x - 9 = 0$

5. $-2x^2 - 5x - 4 = 0$　　　　　**6.** $3x^2 + 2x - 16 = 0$

EXAMPLE 2　*Finding the Number of x-Intercepts*

Determine whether the graph of $y = 7x^2 - 5x + 1$ will intersect the x-axis in *zero*, *one*, or *two* points.

SOLUTION

Let $y = 0$. Then find the value of the discriminant of $7x^2 - 5x + 1 = 0$.

$7x^2 - 5x + 1 = 0$　　　　Identify $a = 7$, $b = -5$, $c = 1$.

$b^2 - 4ac = (-5)^2 - 4(7)(1)$　　Substitute values for a, b, and c.

$\qquad\qquad = 25 - 28$　　　　Simplify.

$\qquad\qquad = -3$　　　　　Discriminant is negative.

The discriminant is negative, so the equation has no real solution. The graph of $y = 7x^2 - 5x + 1$ will intersect the x-axis in zero points.

Algebra 1, Concepts and Skills
Practice Workbook with Examples

NAME _____ DATE _____

Practice with Examples
For use with pages 540–545

Exercises for Example 2

Determine whether the graph of the function will intersect the *x*-axis in *zero*, *one*, or *two* points.

    7. $y = x^2 - 8x + 16$

    8. $y = x^2 - 8x - 1$

    9. $y = x^2 - 8x + 18$

    10. $y = 2x^2 - 6x + 3$

    11. $y = -x^2 + 5x - 8$

    12. $y = 4x^2 + 12x + 9$

Practice with Examples

For use with pages 546–552

GOAL Sketch the graph of a quadratic inequality in two variables.

EXAMPLE 1 *Checking Solutions*

Decide whether the ordered pairs $(-4, -5)$ and $(0, 2)$ are solutions of the inequality $y < x^2 + 5x$.

SOLUTION

$y < x^2 + 5x$	Write original inequality.
$-5 \overset{?}{<} (-4)^2 + 5(-4)$	Substitute -4 for x and -5 for y.
$-5 < -4$	True.

Because $-5 < -4$, the ordered pair $(-4, -5)$ is a solution of the inequality.

$y < x^2 + 5x$	Write original inequality.
$2 \overset{?}{<} (0)^2 + 5(0)$	Substitute 0 for x and 2 for y.
$2 \not< 0$	False.

Because 2 is not less than 0, the ordered pair $(0, 2)$ is not a solution.

Exercises for Example 1

Decide whether the ordered pair is a solution of the inequality.

1. $y \geq x^2 - 2x, \ (2, 0)$

2. $y < 2x^2 + x, \ (1, -1)$

3. $y > x^2 - 3x, \ (2, -3)$

Practice with Examples

For use with pages 546–552

EXAMPLE 2 *Graphing a Quadratic Inequality*

Sketch the graph of $y > -x^2 + 2x - 1$.

SOLUTION

Sketch the graph of the equation $y = -x^2 + 2x - 1$ that corresponds to the inequality $y > -x^2 + 2x - 1$. Use a dashed line because the inequality is $>$. The parabola opens down. Test the point $(0, -2)$ which is *not* on the parabola.

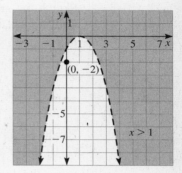

$$y > -x^2 + 2x - 1 \quad \text{Write original inequality.}$$

$$-2 > 0 + 0 - 1 \quad \text{Substitute 0 for } x \text{ and } -2 \text{ for } y.$$

$$-2 \not> -1 \quad \quad -2 \text{ is not greater than } -1.$$

Because -2 is *not* greater than -1, the ordered pair $(0, -2)$ is not a solution. Since the point $(0, 2)$ is a solution and is outside the parabola, the graph of $y > -x^2 + 2x - 1$ is all the points outside the parabola.

Exercises for Example 2

Sketch the graph of the inequality.

4. $y < -x^2$

5. $y > 2x^2 + 1$

6. $y > -x^2 - 3x + 2$

Practice with Examples

For use with pages 546–552

EXAMPLE 3 *Graphing a Quadratic Inequality*

Sketch the graph of $y \geq 2x^2 + 6x$.

SOLUTION

Sketch the graph of the equation $y = 2x^2 + 6x$. Use a solid
line because the inequality is $\geq$. The parabola opens up. Test
the point $(2, 0)$ which is *not* on the parabola.

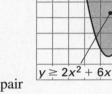

$y \geq 2x^2 + 6x$ Write original inequality.

$0 \overset{?}{\geq} 2(2)^2 + 6(2)$ Substitute 2 for x and 0 for y.

$0 \not\geq 20$ False.

Because 0 is not greater than or equal to 20, the ordered pair
$(2, 0)$ is not a solution.

Since the point $(2, 0)$ is not a solution and it is outside the parabola, the
graph of $y \geq 2x^2 + 6x$ is all the points inside or on the parabola.

Exercises for Example 3
....

Sketch the graph of the inequality.

7. $y \leq x^2 + 4x + 4$

8. $y \geq 3x^2 - 12$

9. $y \leq x^2 - 10x + 9$

LESSON 10.1

Practice with Examples

For use with pages 567–573

GOAL Add and subtract polynomials.

VOCABULARY

A **monomial in one variable** is a number, a variable, or a product of numbers and variables.

A **polynomial** is a monomial or a sum of monomials.

A polynomial is written in **standard form** when the terms are placed in descending order, from largest exponent to smallest exponent.

The **degree** of each term of a polynomial is the exponent of the variable.

The **degree of a polynomial in one variable** is the largest exponent of that variable.

A **binomial** is a polynomial of two terms.

A **trinomial** is a polynomial of three terms.

EXAMPLE 1 *Identifying Polynomials*

Identify the polynomial by degree and by the number of terms.

  a. -2

  b. $2x^2 - 5$

  c. $x^3 + x - 8$

  d. $\frac{1}{2}x$

SOLUTION

  a. constant; monomial

  b. quadratic; binomial

  c. cubic; trinomial

  d. linear; monomial

Exercises for Example 1

Identify the polynomial by degree and by the number of terms.

1. $5x^3$

2. $-x^2 + 4x + 6$

3. $-7 + 3x$

4. $8x^2$

Practice with Examples

For use with pages 567–573

EXAMPLE 2 *Adding Polynomials*

Find the sum and write the answer in standard form.

a. $(6x - x^2 + 3) + (4x^2 - x - 2)$ **b.** $(x^2 - x - 4) + (2x + 3x^2 + 1)$

SOLUTION

a. Vertical format: Write each expression in standard form. Line up like terms.

$$-x^2 + 6x + 3$$
$$\underline{4x^2 - x - 2}$$
$$3x^2 + 5x + 1$$

b. Horizontal format: Group like terms.

$$(x^2 - x - 4) + (2x + 3x^2 + 1) = (x^2 + 3x^2) + (-x + 2x) + (-4 + 1)$$
$$= 4x^2 + x - 3$$

Exercises for Example 2

Find the sum. Write the answer in standard form.

5. $(7 + 2x - 4x^2) + (-3x + x^2 - 5)$

6. $(8x - 9 + 2x^2) + (1 + x - 6x^2)$

Practice with Examples

For use with pages 567–573

EXAMPLE 3 *Subtracting Polynomials*

Find the difference and write the answer in standard form.

a. $(5x^2 - 4x + 1) - (8 - x^2)$ **b.** $(-x + 2x^2) - (3x^2 + 7x - 2)$

SOLUTION

a. Vertical format: To subtract, you add the opposite.

$$(5x^2 - 4x + 1) \qquad\qquad\qquad 5x^2 - 4x + 1$$
$$\underline{-\qquad(8 - x^2)} \quad \text{Add the opposite.} \quad \underline{+\ x^2 \qquad\quad - 8}$$
$$\qquad\qquad\qquad\qquad\qquad\qquad\qquad\qquad 6x^2 - 4x - 7$$

b. Horizontal format: Group like terms and simplify.

$$(-x + 2x^2) - (3x^2 + 7x - 2) = -x + 2x^2 - 3x^2 - 7x + 2$$
$$= (2x^2 - 3x^2) + (-x - 7x) + 2$$
$$= -x^2 - 8x + 2$$

Exercises for Example 3

Find the difference. Write the answer in standard form.

7. $(x + 7x^2) - (1 + 3x - x^2)$

8. $(2x + 3 - 5x^2) - (2x^2 - x + 6)$

Practice with Examples

For use with pages 574–580

GOAL **Multiply polynomials.**

> **VOCABULARY**
>
> To multiply two binomials, use a pattern called the **FOIL** pattern.
> Multiply the First, Outer, Inner, and Last terms.

EXAMPLE 1 **Multiplying Binomials Using the FOIL Pattern**

Find the product $(4x + 3)(x + 2)$.

SOLUTION

$$
\begin{array}{cccc}
\text{F} & \text{O} & \text{I} & \text{L} \\
\downarrow & \downarrow & \downarrow & \downarrow
\end{array}
$$

$$(4x + 3)(x + 2) = 4x^2 + 8x + 3x + 6$$

$$\qquad\qquad\qquad = 4x^2 + 11x + 6 \qquad \text{Combine like terms.}$$

Exercises for Example 1

Use the FOIL pattern to find the product.

1. $(2x + 3)(x + 1)$ **2.** $(y - 2)(y - 3)$ **3.** $(3a + 2)(2a - 1)$

EXAMPLE 2 **Multiplying Polynomials Vertically**

Find the product $(x + 3)(4 - 2x^2 + x)$.

SOLUTION

To multiply two polynomials that have three or more terms, you must multiply each term
of one polynomial by each term of the other polynomial. Align like terms vertically.

$$
\begin{array}{rl}
\begin{array}{r}
-2x^2 + x + 4 \\
\times x + 3 \\
\hline
-6x^2 + 3x + 12 \\
-2x^3 + x^2 + 4x \\
\hline
-2x^3 - 5x^2 + 7x + 12
\end{array}
&
\begin{array}{l}
\text{Standard form} \\
\text{Standard form} \\
3(-2x^2 + x + 4) \\
x(-2x^2 + x + 4) \\
\text{Combine like terms.}
\end{array}
\end{array}
$$

Practice with Examples

For use with pages 574–580

Exercises for Example 2

Multiply the polynomials vertically.

4. $(a + 4)(a^2 + 3 - 2a)$

5. $(2y + 1)(y^2 - 5 + y)$

EXAMPLE 3 *Multiplying Polynomials Horizontally*

Find the product $(x + 4)(-2x^2 + 3x - 1)$.

SOLUTION

Multiply $-2x^2 + 3x - 1$ by each term of $x + 4$.

$$(x + 4)(-2x^2 + 3x - 1) = x(-2x^2 + 3x - 1) + 4(-2x^2 + 3x - 1)$$
$$= -2x^3 + 3x^2 - x - 8x^2 + 12x - 4$$
$$= -2x^3 - 5x^2 + 11x - 4$$

Exercises for Example 3

Multiply the polynomials horizontally.

6. $(a + 4)(a^2 + 3 - 2a)$

7. $(2y + 1)(y^2 - 5 + y)$

NAME _____ DATE _____

Practice with Examples

For use with pages 574–580

EXAMPLE 4 *Multiplying Binomials to Find an Area*

The dimensions of a rectangular garden can be represented by a width of $(x + 6)$ feet and a length of $(2x + 5)$ feet. Write a polynomial expression for the area A of the garden.

SOLUTION

The area model for a rectangle is $A = $ (width)(length).

$$
\begin{aligned}
A &= \text{(width)(length)} && \text{Area model for a rectangle} \\
&= (x + 6)(2x + 5) && \text{Substitute } x + 6 \text{ for width and } 2x + 5 \text{ for length.} \\
&= 2x^2 + 5x + 12x + 30 && \text{Use FOIL pattern.} \\
&= 2x^2 + 17x + 30 && \text{Combine like terms.}
\end{aligned}
$$

The area A of the garden can be represented by $2x^2 + 17x + 30$.

Exercise for Example 4
....

8. Rework Example 4 if the width is $(x + 3)$ feet and the length is $(3x + 2)$ feet.

NAME _____ DATE _____

Practice with Examples

For use with pages 581–587

GOAL Use special product patterns to multiply polynomials.

VOCABULARY

Some pairs of binomials have **special product** patterns as follows.

Sum and Difference Pattern

$(a + b)(a - b) = a^2 - b^2$

Square of a Binomial Pattern

$(a + b)^2 = a^2 + 2ab + b^2$

$(a - b)^2 = a^2 - 2ab + b^2$

EXAMPLE 1 *Using the Sum and Difference Pattern*

Use the sum and difference pattern to find the product $(4y + 3)(4y - 3)$.

SOLUTION

$\quad (a + b)(a - b) = a^2 - b^2$ Write pattern.

$(4y + 3)(4y - 3) = (4y)^2 - 3^2$ Apply pattern.

$\quad\quad\quad\quad\quad\quad = 16y^2 - 9$ Simplify.

Exercises for Example 1

Use the sum and difference pattern to find the product.

1. $(x + 5)(x - 5)$

2. $(3x + 2)(3x - 2)$

3. $(x + 2)(x - 2)$

Practice with Examples

For use with pages 581–587

EXAMPLE 2 *Squaring a Binomial*

Use the square of a binomial pattern to find the product.

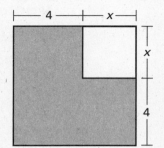

a. $(2x + 3)^2$ **b.** $(4x - 1)^2$

SOLUTION

a. $(a + b)^2 = a^2 + 2ab + b^2$ Write pattern.

     $(2x + 3)^2 = (2x)^2 + 2(2x)(3) + 3^2$ Apply pattern.

               $= 4x^2 + 12x + 9$ Simplify.

b. $(a - b)^2 = a^2 - 2ab + b^2$ Write pattern.

     $(4x - 1)^2 = (4x)^2 - 2(4x)(1) + 1^2$ Apply pattern.

               $= 16x^2 - 8x + 1$ Simplify.

Exercises for Example 2

Use the square of a binomial pattern to find the product.

4. $(m + 3)^2$

5. $(3x - 2)^2$

6. $(7y + 2)^2$

NAME _____ DATE _____

Practice with Examples

For use with pages 581–587

EXAMPLE 3 *Finding the Area of a Figure*

Use a special product pattern to find an expression for the area of the shaded region.

SOLUTION

Verbal Model	Area of shaded region	=

	Area of entire square	−	Area of smaller square

Labels Area of shaded region = A (square units)

Area of entire square = $(x + 4)^2$ (square units)

Area of smaller square = x^2 (square units)

Algebraic Model

$$A = (x + 4)^2 - x^2 \qquad \text{Write algebraic model.}$$
$$= (x^2 + 8x + 16) - x^2 \qquad \text{Apply pattern.}$$
$$= 8x + 16 \qquad \text{Simplify.}$$

The area of the shaded region can be represented by $8x + 16$ square units.

Exercises for Example 3

7. Use a special product pattern to find an expression for the area of the shaded region.

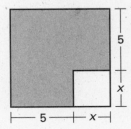

8. Use a special product pattern to find an expression for the area of the shaded region.

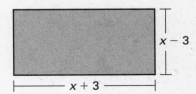

Practice with Examples

For use with pages 588–593

GOAL **Solve quadratic equations in factored form.**

> ### VOCABULARY
>
> A polynomial is in **factored form** if it is written as the product of two or more linear factors. According to the **zero-product property,** if the product of two factors is zero, then at least one of the factors must be zero.

EXAMPLE 1 *Solving a Factored Equation*

Solve the equation $(x - 1)(x + 7) = 0$.

SOLUTION

Use the zero-product property: either $x - 1 = 0$ or $x + 7 = 0$.

$(x - 1)(x + 7) = 0$ Write original equation.

$x - 1 = 0$ Set first factor equal to 0.

$x = 1$ Solve for x.

$x + 7 = 0$ Set second factor equal to 0.

$x = -7$ Solve for x.

The solutions are 1 and -7.

Exercises for Example 1

Solve the equation.

1. $(z - 6)(z + 6) = 0$

2. $(y - 5)(y - 1) = 0$

3. $(x + 4)(x + 3) = 0$

Practice with Examples

For use with pages 588–593

EXAMPLE 2 *Solving a Repeated–Factor Equation*

Solve the equation $(x - 4)^2 = 0$.

SOLUTION

This equation has a repeated factor. To solve the equation, you just set $x - 4$ equal to zero.

$(x - 4)^2 = 0$	Write original equation.
$x - 4 = 0$	Set repeated factor equal to 0.
$x = 4$	Solve for x.

The solution is 4.

Exercises for Example 2

Solve the equation.

4. $(t - 5)^2 = 0$

5. $(y + 3)^2 = 0$

6. $(2x + 4)^2 = 0$

Algebra 1, Concepts and Skills
Practice Workbook with Examples

NAME _____ DATE _____

Practice with Examples
For use with pages 588–593

EXAMPLE 3 *Graphing a Factored Equation*

Name the x-intercepts and the vertex of the graph
of the function $y = (x + 4)(x - 2)$. Then sketch
the graph of the function.

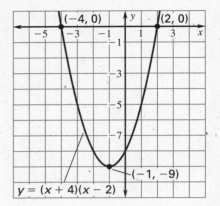

SOLUTION

First solve $(x + 4)(x - 2) = 0$ to find the
x-intercepts: -4 and 2.

Then find the coordinates of the vertex.

• The x-coordinate of the vertex is the average
of the x-intercepts.

$$x = \frac{-4 + 2}{2} = -1$$

• Substitute to find the y-coordinate.

$$y = (-1 + 4)(-1 - 2) = -9$$

• The coordinates of the vertex are $(-1, -9)$.

Exercises for Example 3

**Name the x-intercepts and the vertex of the graph of the
function.**

7. $y = (x + 3)(x + 1)$

8. $y = (x - 2)(x - 4)$

9. $y = (x - 1)(x + 5)$

NAME _____ DATE _____

Practice with Examples

For use with pages 594–601

GOAL Factor trinomials of the form $x^2 + bx + c$.

VOCABULARY

To **factor a trinomial** means to write it as the product of two binomials. To factor $x^2 + bx + c$, you need to find numbers p and q such that

$$p + q = b \quad \text{and} \quad pq = c.$$

$x^2 + bx + c = (x + p)(x + q)$ when $p + q = b$ and $pq = c$

EXAMPLE 1 *Factoring when b and c Are Positive*

Factor $x^2 + 6x + 8$.

SOLUTION

For this trinomial, $b = 6$ and $c = 8$. You need to find two numbers whose sum is 6 and whose product is 8.

$$x^2 + 6x + 8 = (x + p)(x + q) \qquad \text{Find } p \text{ and } q \text{ when } p + q = 6 \text{ and } pq = 8.$$
$$= (x + 4)(x + 2) \qquad p = 4 \text{ and } q = 2$$

Exercises for Example 1
....
Factor the trinomial.

1. $x^2 + 5x + 6$

2. $x^2 + 6x + 5$

3. $x^2 + 3x + 2$

NAME _____ DATE _____

Practice with Examples

For use with pages 594–601

EXAMPLE 3 *Factoring when b Is Negative and c Is Positive*

Factor $x^2 - 5x + 4$.

SOLUTION

Because b is negative and c is positive, both p and q must be negative numbers. Find two numbers whose sum is -5 and whose product is 4.

$$x^2 - 5x + 4 = (x + p)(x + q) \qquad \text{Find } p \text{ and } q \text{ when } p + q = -5 \text{ and } pq = 4.$$
$$= (x - 4)(x - 1) \qquad p = -4 \text{ and } q = -1$$

Exercises for Example 2

Factor the trinomial.

4. $x^2 - 3x + 2$

5. $x^2 - 7x + 12$

6. $x^2 - 5x + 6$

EXAMPLE 2 *Factoring when b and c Are Negative*

Factor $x^2 - 3x - 10$.

SOLUTION

For this trinomial, $b = -3$ and $c = -10$. Because c is negative, you need to find numbers p and q with different signs.

$$x^2 - 3x - 10 = (x + p)(x + q) \qquad \text{Find } p \text{ and } q \text{ when } p + q = -3 \text{ and } pq = -10.$$
$$= (x + 2)(x - 5) \qquad p = 2 \text{ and } q = -5$$

Exercises for Example 3

Factor the trinomial.

7. $x^2 - x - 2$

8. $x^2 - 4x - 12$

9. $x^2 - 2x - 8$

Algebra 1, Concepts and Skills
Practice Workbook with Examples

NAME _____ DATE _____

Practice with Examples

For use with pages 594–601

EXAMPLE 4 *Solving a Quadratic Equation*

Solve $x^2 + 4x = 12$ by factoring.

SOLUTION

$x^2 + 4x = 12$	Write equation.
$x^2 + 4x - 12 = 0$	Write in standard form.
$(x + 6)(x - 2) = 0$	Factor left side. Because c is negative, you need to find numbers p and q with different signs. So, $p = 6$ and $q = -2$.
$x + 6 = 0$ or $x - 2 = 0$	Use zero-product property.
$x + 6 = 0$	Set first factor equal to 0.
$x = -6$	Solve for x.
$x - 2 = 0$	Set second factor equal to 0.
$x = 2$	Solve for x.

The solutions are -6 and 2.

Exercises for Example 4

Solve the equation by factoring.

10. $x^2 + 8x + 15 = 0$

11. $x^2 - 8x + 12 = 0$

12. $x^2 + 3x - 4 = 0$

NAME _____ DATE _____

Practice with Examples

For use with pages 602–608

GOAL Factor trinomials of the form $ax^2 + bx + c$.

VOCABULARY

To factor a trinomial of the form $ax^2 + bx + c$, find the factors of a (m and n) and the factors of c (p and q) so that the sum of the outer and inner products (mq and pn) is b.

$$c = pq$$
$$ax^2 + bx + c = (mx + p)(nx + q) \qquad b = mq + pn$$
$$a = mn$$

EXAMPLE 1 *Factoring when a and c Are Prime Numbers*

Factor $3x^2 + 7x + 2$.

SOLUTION

Test the possible factors of a (1 and 3) and c (1 and 2).

Try $a = 1 \cdot 3$ and $c = 1 \cdot 2$.

$\qquad (1x + 1)(3x + 2) = 3x^2 + 5x + 2 \qquad$ Not correct

Try $a = 1 \cdot 3$ and $c = 2 \cdot 1$.

$\qquad (1x + 2)(3x + 1) = 3x^2 + 7x + 2 \qquad$ Correct

The correct factorization of $3x^2 + 7x + 2$ is $(x + 2)(3x + 1)$.

Exercises for Example 1
Factor the trinomial.

1. $5x^2 + 11x + 2$

2. $2x^2 + 5x + 3$

3. $3x^2 + 10x + 7$

Algebra 1, Concepts and Skills
Practice Workbook with Examples

Practice with Examples

For use with pages 602–608

EXAMPLE 2 *Factoring when a and c Are not Prime Numbers*

Factor $4x^2 - 13x + 10$.

SOLUTION

Both factors of c must be negative, because b is negative and c is positive.

Test the possible factors of a and c.

FACTORS OF a AND c	PRODUCT	CORRECT?
$a = 1 \cdot 4$ and $c = (-1)(-10)$	$(x - 1)(4x - 10) = 4x^2 - 14x + 10$	No
$a = 1 \cdot 4$ and $c = (-10)(-1)$	$(x - 10)(4x - 1) = 4x^2 - 41x + 10$	No
$a = 1 \cdot 4$ and $c = (-2)(-5)$	$(x - 2)(4x - 5) = 4x^2 - 13x + 10$	Yes

The correct factorization of $4x^2 - 13x + 10$ is $(x - 2)(4x - 5)$.

Exercises for Example 2

Factor the trinomial.

4. $9x^2 + 65x + 14$

5. $6x^2 - 23x + 15$

6. $8x^2 + 38x + 9$

Algebra 1, Concepts and Skills
Practice Workbook with Examples

NAME _____ DATE _____

Practice with Examples

For use with pages 602–608

EXAMPLE 3 *Solving a Quadratic Equation*

Solve the equation $3x^2 - x = 10$ by factoring.

SOLUTION

$3x^2 - x = 10$	Write equation.
$3x^2 - x - 10 = 0$	Write in standard form.
$(3x + 5)(x - 2) = 0$	Factor left side.
$3x + 5 = 0$ or $x - 2 = 0$	Use zero-product property.
$3x + 5 = 0$	Set first factor equal to 0.
$x = -\frac{5}{3}$	Solve for x.
$x - 2 = 0$	Set second factor equal to 0.
$x = 2$	Solve for x.

The solutions are $-\frac{5}{3}$ and 2.

Exercises for Example 3

Solve the equation by factoring.

7. $2x^2 + 7x + 3 = 0$

8. $5n^2 - 17n = -6$

9. $6x^2 - x - 2 = 0$

Algebra 1, Concepts and Skills
Practice Workbook with Examples

NAME _____ DATE _____

Practice with Examples

For use with pages 609–615

GOAL Factor special products.

VOCABULARY

Factoring Special Products

Difference of Two Squares Pattern   **Example**
$a^2 - b^2 = (a + b)(a - b)$ $9x^2 - 16 = (3x + 4)(3x - 4)$

Perfect Square Trinomial Pattern   **Example**
$a^2 + 2ab + b^2 = (a + b)^2$ $x^2 + 8x + 16 = (x + 4)^2$
$a^2 - 2ab + b^2 = (a - b)^2$ $x^2 - 12x + 36 = (x - 6)^2$

EXAMPLE 1 *Factoring the Difference of Two Squares*

a. $n^2 - 25$ **b.** $4x^2 - y^2$

SOLUTION

a. $n^2 - 25 = n^2 - 5^2$ Write as $a^2 - b^2$.
$\qquad = (n + 5)(n - 5)$ Factor using difference of two squares pattern.
b. $4x^2 - y^2 = (2x)^2 - y^2$ Write as $a^2 - b^2$.
$\qquad = (2x + y)(2x - y)$ Factor using difference of two squares pattern.

Exercises for Example 1
···

Factor the expression.

1. $16 - 9y^2$ **2.** $4q^2 - 49$ **3.** $36 - 25x^2$

EXAMPLE 2 *Factoring Perfect Square Trinomials*

a. $x^2 - 6x + 9$ **b.** $9y^2 + 12y + 4$

SOLUTION

a. $x^2 - 6x + 9 = x^2 - 2(x)(3) + 3^2$ Write as $a^2 - 2ab + b^2$.
$\qquad = (x - 3)^2$ Factor using perfect square trinomial pattern.

b. $9y^2 + 12y + 4 = (3y)^2 + 2(3y)(2) + 2^2$ Write as $a^2 + 2ab + b^2$.
$\qquad = (3y + 2)^2$ Factor using perfect square trinomial pattern.

Exercises for Example 2
···

Factor the expression.

4. $x^2 - 18x + 81$ **5.** $4n^2 + 20n + 25$ **6.** $16y^2 + 8y + 1$

NAME _____ DATE _____

Practice with Examples

For use with pages 609–615

EXAMPLE 3 **Solving a Quadratic Equation**

Solve the equation $2x^2 - 28x + 98 = 0$.

SOLUTION

$2x^2 - 28x + 98 = 0$	Write original equation.
$2(x^2 - 14x + 49) = 0$	Factor out common factor.
$2[x^2 - 2(7x) + 7^2] = 0$	Write as $a^2 - 2ab + b^2$.
$2(x - 7)^2 = 0$	Factor using perfect square trinomial pattern.
$x - 7 = 0$	Set repeated factor equal to 0.
$x = 7$	Solve for x.

The solution is 7.

Exercises for Example 3

Use factoring to solve the equation.

7. $x^2 - 20x + 100 = 0$

8. $4n^2 - 4n = -1$

9. $3z^2 - 24z + 48 = 0$

Algebra 1, Concepts and Skills
Practice Workbook with Examples

NAME _____ DATE _____

Practice with Examples

For use with pages 609–615

EXAMPLE 4 *Solving a Quadratic Equation*

Solve the equation $75 - 48x^2 = 0$.

SOLUTION

$75 - 48x^2 = 0$	Write original equation.
$3(25 - 16x^2) = 0$	Factor out common factor.
$3[5^2 - (4x)^2] = 0$	Write as $a^2 - b^2$.
$3(5 + 4x)(5 - 4x) = 0$	Factor using difference of two squares pattern.
$5 + 4x = 0$ or $5 - 4x = 0$	Use zero-product property.
$5 + 4x = 0$	Set first factor equal to 0.
$x = -\frac{5}{4}$	Solve for x.
$5 - 4x = 0$	Set second factor equal to 0.
$x = \frac{5}{4}$	Solve for x.

The solutions are $-\frac{5}{4}$ and $\frac{5}{4}$.

Exercises for Example 4

Use factoring to solve the equation.

10. $x^2 - 49 = 0$

11. $9y^2 - 64 = 0$

12. $4x^2 = 81$

Practice with Examples

For use with pages 616–622

GOAL **Factor cubic polynomials.**

VOCABULARY

A polynomial is **prime** if it cannot be factored using integer coefficients.

To **factor a polynomial completely**, write it as a product of a monomial and prime polynomials.

EXAMPLE 1 *Finding the Greatest Common Factor*

Factor the greatest common factor out of $8x^4 - 24x^2$.

SOLUTION

Write each term using prime factors.

$8x^4 = 2^3 \cdot x^4$ $\qquad\qquad$ $24x^2 = 2^3 \cdot 3 \cdot x^2$

$2^3 x^2$ is the greatest common factor.

Use the distributive property to factor out the greatest common factor from each term.

$8x^4 - 24x^2 = 8x^2(x^2 - 3)$

Exercises for Example 1

Factor out the greatest common factor.

1. $5x^2 + 10x$

2. $4x^4 + 6x^3 + 14x$

3. $12x^5 + 6x^3 - 3x^2$

Practice with Examples

For use with pages 616–622

EXAMPLE 2 *Factoring Completely*

Factor $8x^2 - 32$ completely.

SOLUTION

$$8x^2 - 32 = 8(x^2 - 4) \qquad \text{Factor out the greatest common factor, 8.}$$
$$= 8(x - 2)(x + 2) \qquad \text{Factor the difference of two squares.}$$

Exercises for Example 2

Factor the expression completely.

4. $48a^3 - 3a^2$

5. $2a^2 - 2$

6. $2x^3 + 14x^2 + 20x$

7. $4n^4 - 28n^3 + 40n^2$

EXAMPLE 3 *Factoring by Grouping*

Factor $x^3 + 4x^2 - 9x - 36$ completely.

SOLUTION

$$x^3 + 4x^2 - 9x - 36 = (x^3 + 4x^2) + (-9x - 36) \qquad \text{Group terms.}$$
$$= x^2(x + 4) - 9(x + 4) \qquad \text{Factor each group.}$$
$$= (x^2 - 9)(x + 4) \qquad \text{Use distributive property.}$$
$$= (x + 3)(x - 3)(x + 4) \qquad \text{Factor difference of two squares.}$$

Exercises for Example 3

Use grouping to factor the expression completely.

8. $x^3 - 3x^2 - 4x + 12$

9. $2x^3 + 10x^2 - 8x - 40$

10. $6x^3 - 24x^2 + 9x - 36$

11. $5x^3 - 20x^2 - 45x + 180$

Practice with Examples

For use with pages 616–622

EXAMPLE 4 *Factoring the Sum or Difference of Two Cubes*

Factor: **a.** $x^3 + 8$ **b.** $a^3 - 64$

SOLUTION

a. $x^3 + 8 = x^3 + 2^3$ Write as a sum of two cubes.

$= (x + 2)(x^2 - 2x + 4)$ Use special product pattern.

b. $a^3 - 64 = a^3 - 4^3$ Write as a difference of two cubes.

$= (a - 4)(a^2 + 4a + 16)$ Use special product pattern.

Exercises for Example 4

Factor.

12. $8y^3 + 27$

13. $x^3 + 64$

14. $8x^3 + 125$

15. $27y^3 - 1$

16. $8y^3 - 27$

17. $x^3 - 343$

Practice with Examples

For use with pages 633–638

GOAL **Solve proportions.**

VOCABULARY

A **proportion** is an equation that states that two ratios are equal. In the proportion $\frac{a}{b} = \frac{c}{d}$, the numbers a and d are the **extremes** of the proportion and the numbers b and c are the **means** of the proportion.

Properties of Proportions

Reciprocal Property

If two ratios are equal, their reciprocals are also equal.

If $\frac{a}{b} = \frac{c}{d}$, then $\frac{b}{a} = \frac{d}{c}$.

Cross Product Property

The product of the extremes equals the product of the means.

If $\frac{a}{b} = \frac{c}{d}$, then $ad = bc$.

Solving for the variable in a proportion is called **solving the proportion.**

EXAMPLE 1 *Using the Cross Product Property and Checking Solutions*

Solve the proportion $\frac{x^2 - 4}{x + 2} = \frac{x - 2}{2}$.

SOLUTION

$\frac{x^2 - 4}{x + 2} = \frac{x - 2}{2}$ Write original proportion.

$2(x^2 - 4) = (x + 2)(x - 2)$ Use cross product property. $\frac{x^2 - 4}{x + 2} \diagdown\!\!\!\!\diagup \frac{x - 2}{2}$

$2x^2 - 8 = x^2 - 4$ Use distributive property and simplify.

$x^2 = 4$ Isolate variable term.

$x = \pm 2$ Take square root of each side.

The solutions appear to be $x = 2$ and $x = -2$. You must check each solution in the original proportion to eliminate any values that result in a zero denominator.

NAME _____ DATE _____

Practice with Examples

For use with pages 633–638

$x = 2$:

$$\frac{x^2 - 4}{x + 2} = \frac{x - 2}{2}$$

$$\frac{2^2 - 4}{2 + 2} \stackrel{?}{=} \frac{2 - 2}{2}$$

$$\frac{0}{4} \stackrel{?}{=} \frac{0}{2}$$

$$0 = 0$$

$x = -2$:

$$\frac{x^2 - 4}{x + 2} = \frac{x - 2}{2}$$

$$\frac{(-2)^2 - 4}{(-2) + 2} \stackrel{?}{=} \frac{(-2) - 2}{2}$$

$$\frac{0}{0} \stackrel{\cancel{=}}{} \frac{-4}{2}$$

You can conclude that $x = -2$ is not a solution because the check results in a false statement. The only solution is $x = 2$.

Exercises for Example 1

Solve the proportion and check your solutions.

1. $\dfrac{4}{x} = \dfrac{x}{16}$

2. $\dfrac{x + 5}{6} = \dfrac{x - 2}{4}$

3. $\dfrac{x - 1}{2} = \dfrac{x^2 - 1}{x + 1}$

Algebra 1, Concepts and Skills
Practice Workbook with Examples

Practice with Examples

For use with pages 633–638

EXAMPLE 2 **Writing and Using a Proportion**

You are making a scale model of a sailboat. The boat is 20 feet long and 15 feet high. Your scale model will be 12 inches high. How long should it be?

SOLUTION

Let L represent the length of the model.

$$\frac{\text{Length of actual boat}}{\text{Height of actual boat}} = \frac{\text{Length of model}}{\text{Height of model}}$$

$$\frac{20}{15} = \frac{L}{12}$$

The solution is $L = 16$. Your scale model should be 16 inches long.

Exercise for Example 2

4. Rework Example 2 if your scale model is 18 inches high.

Practice with Examples

For use with pages 639–645

GOAL **Use direct and inverse variation.**

VOCABULARY

The variables x and y vary **directly** if for a constant k

$\dfrac{y}{x} = k$, or $y = kx$, where $k \neq 0$.

The variables x and y vary **inversely** if for a constant k

$xy = k$, or $y = \dfrac{k}{x}$, where $k \neq 0$.

The number k is the **constant of variation.**

EXAMPLE 1 *Use Direct and Inverse Variation*

_____

When x is 4, y is 6. Find an equation that relates x and y in each case.

a. x and y vary directly.   **b.** x and y vary inversely.

SOLUTION

a. $\dfrac{y}{x} = k$ Write direct variation model.

    $\dfrac{6}{4} = k$ Substitute 4 for x and 6 for y.

    $\dfrac{3}{2} = k$ Simplify.

The direct variation equation that relates x and y is $\dfrac{y}{x} = \dfrac{3}{2}$, or $y = \dfrac{3}{2}x$.

b. $xy = k$ Write inverse variation model.

    $(4)(6) = k$ Substitute 4 for x and 6 for y.

       $24 = k$ Simplify.

An equation that relates x and y is $xy = 24$, or $y = \dfrac{24}{x}$.

Practice with Examples

For use with pages 639–645

Exercises for Example 1

When x is 4, y is 5. Find an equation that relates x and y in each case.

1. x and y vary directly.

2. x and y vary inversely.

EXAMPLE 2 *Write and Use a Model*

The graph at the right shows a model for the relationship between the length of a particular rectangle and the width of the rectangle if the area of the rectangle is fixed. For the values shown, the length ℓ and the width w vary inversely.

a. Find an inverse variation model that relates ℓ and w.

b. Use the model to find the length for a width of 8 inches.

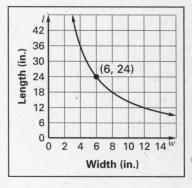

SOLUTION

a. From the graph, you can see that $\ell = 24$ inches when $w = 6$ inches.

$\ell = \dfrac{k}{w}$ Write inverse variation model.

$24 = \dfrac{k}{6}$ Substitute 24 for ℓ and 6 for w.

$144 = k$ Solve for k.

The model is $\ell = \dfrac{144}{w}$, where ℓ and w are in inches.

b. When $w = 8$ inches, $\ell = \dfrac{144}{8} = 18$ inches.

Algebra 1, Concepts and Skills
Practice Workbook with Examples

NAME _____ DATE _____

Practice with Examples

For use with pages 639–645

Exercises for Example 2

3. Use the model in Example 2 to find the length of a rectangle for a width of 4 inches.

4. Suppose the length and width of a rectangle vary inversely. When the length is 16 inches, the width is 8 inches. Find an inverse variation model that relates the length and width if the area is fixed.

5. Using your answer to Exercise 4, find the length of the rectangle when the width is 2, 4, 16, and 20 inches.

Algebra 1, Concepts and Skills
Practice Workbook with Examples

NAME _____ DATE _____

Practice with Examples

For use with pages 646–651

GOAL Simplify rational expressions.

VOCABULARY

A **rational number** is a number that can be written as the quotient of two integers.

A **rational expression** is a fraction whose numerator and denominator are nonzero polynomials.

A rational expression is in **simplest form** if its numerator and denominator have no factors in common (other than ± 1).

EXAMPLE 1 *Simplify a Rational Expression*

Simplify the expression if possible.

a. $\dfrac{x^2 - 5}{x}$ b. $\dfrac{x^2 - 6x}{3x^2}$

SOLUTION

a. When you simplify rational expressions, you can divide out only factors, not terms. You cannot simplify $\dfrac{x^2 - 5}{x}$. You cannot divide out the common term x.

b. $\dfrac{x^2 - 6x}{3x^2} = \dfrac{\cancel{x}(x - 6)}{\cancel{x} \cdot 3x}$ You can divide out the common factor x.

$= \dfrac{x - 6}{3x}$ Simplify.

Exercises for Example 1
....

Simplify the expression if possible.

1. $\dfrac{3x}{4x + x^2}$ 2. $\dfrac{x^2(x - 7)}{x^3}$ 3. $\dfrac{x^3 + 3}{x^3}$

Algebra 1, Concepts and Skills
Practice Workbook with Examples

Practice with Examples

For use with pages 646–651

EXAMPLE 2 *Recognize Opposite Factors*

Simplify $\dfrac{x^2 - 6x + 8}{4 - x}$.

SOLUTION

$$\dfrac{x^2 - 6x + 8}{4 - x} = \dfrac{(x - 2)(x - 4)}{4 - x}$$ Factor numerator and denominator.

$$= \dfrac{(x - 2)(x - 4)}{-(x - 4)}$$ Factor -1 from $(4 - x)$.

$$= \dfrac{(x - 2)(x - 4)}{-(x - 4)}$$ Divide out common factor $(x - 4)$.

$$= -(x - 2)$$ Simplify.

$$= 2 - x$$ Simplify.

Exercises for Example 2

Simplify the expression if possible.

4. $\dfrac{x^2 - 8x + 12}{2 - x}$

5. $\dfrac{1 - x^2}{x^2 - 3x + 2}$

6. $\dfrac{1 - x}{x^2 + 2x - 3}$

Practice with Examples

For use with pages 646–651

EXAMPLE 3 *Divide a Polynomial by a Binomial*

Divide $(4y^2 - 10y - 6)$ by $(y - 3)$.

SOLUTION

$\dfrac{4y^2 - 10y - 6}{y - 3}$ Rewrite the problem as a rational expression.

$\dfrac{2(2y + 1)(y - 3)}{y - 3}$ Factor the numerator.

$\dfrac{2(2y + 1)(y - 3)}{y - 3}$ Divide out the common factor $(y - 3)$.

$4y + 2$ Simplify the expression.

Exercise for Example 3

7. Divide $(6y^2 + 15y - 9)$ by $(y + 3)$.

NAME _____ DATE _____

Practice with Examples

For use with pages 652–657

GOAL **Multiply and divide rational expressions.**

VOCABULARY

Let a, b, c, and d be nonzero polynomials.

To **multiply** rational expressions, multiply numerators and denominators.

$$\frac{a}{b} \cdot \frac{c}{d} = \frac{ac}{bd}$$

To **divide** rational expressions, multiply by the reciprocal of the divisor.

$$\frac{a}{b} \div \frac{c}{d} = \frac{a}{b} \cdot \frac{d}{c}$$

EXAMPLE 1 *Multiply Rational Expressions*

Simplify $\dfrac{x + 3}{x^2 - 4} \cdot \dfrac{x + 2}{x^2 + 4x + 3}$.

SOLUTION

$$\frac{x + 3}{x^2 - 4} \cdot \frac{x + 2}{x^2 + 4x + 3} = \frac{x + 3}{(x + 2)(x - 2)} \cdot \frac{x + 2}{(x + 3)(x + 1)} \quad \text{Factor numerators and denominators.}$$

$$= \frac{(x + 3)(x + 2)}{(x + 2)(x - 2)(x + 3)(x + 1)} \quad \text{Multiply numerators and denominators.}$$

$$= \frac{(x + 3)(x + 2)}{(x + 2)(x - 2)(x + 3)(x + 1)} \quad \text{Divide out common factors.}$$

$$= \frac{1}{(x - 2)(x + 1)} \quad \text{Simplify.}$$

Exercises for Example 1

Simplify the expression.

1. $\dfrac{5x}{x^2 - 2x - 8} \cdot \dfrac{2x - 8}{5x^2}$

Algebra 1, Concepts and Skills
Practice Workbook with Examples

Practice with Examples

For use with pages 652–657

Simplify the expression.

2. $\dfrac{x^2 - 9}{6} \cdot \dfrac{3x + 6}{x^2 - x - 6}$

EXAMPLE 2 *Divide by a Polynomial*

Simplify $\dfrac{x^2 - x - 12}{x^2 - 9} \div (x - 4)$.

SOLUTION

$\dfrac{x^2 - x - 12}{x^2 - 9} \div (x - 4) = \dfrac{x^2 - x - 12}{x^2 - 9} \cdot \dfrac{1}{x - 4}$ Multiply by reciprocal.

$= \dfrac{(x - 4)(x + 3)}{(x + 3)(x - 3)} \cdot \dfrac{1}{(x - 4)}$ Factor.

$= \dfrac{(x - 4)(x + 3)}{(x + 3)(x - 3)(x - 4)}$ Multiply numerators and denominators.

$= \dfrac{\cancel{(x - 4)}\cancel{(x + 3)}}{\cancel{(x + 3)}(x - 3)\cancel{(x - 4)}}$ Divide out common factors.

$= \dfrac{1}{x - 3}$ Simplify.

Exercises for Example 2

Simplify the expression.

3. $\dfrac{x^2 - 49}{x} \div 5(x + 7)$

Practice with Examples

For use with pages 652–657

Simplify the expression.

4. $\dfrac{x^2 - 5x + 4}{x^2} \div (x - 1)$

Algebra 1, Concepts and Skills
Practice Workbook with Examples

Practice with Examples

For use with pages 658–662

GOAL Add and subtract rational expressions with like denominators.

VOCABULARY

Let a, b, and c be polynomials, with $c \neq 0$.

To **add**, add the numerators. $\dfrac{a}{c} + \dfrac{b}{c} = \dfrac{a + b}{c}$

To **subtract**, subtract the numerators. $\dfrac{a}{c} - \dfrac{b}{c} = \dfrac{a - b}{c}$

EXAMPLE 1 *Add Rational Expressions*

Simplify $\dfrac{3x}{x + 2} + \dfrac{5x + 1}{x + 2}$.

SOLUTION

$$\dfrac{3x}{x + 2} + \dfrac{5x + 1}{x + 2} = \dfrac{3x + (5x + 1)}{x + 2} \qquad \text{Add the numerators.}$$

$$= \dfrac{8x + 1}{x + 2} \qquad \text{Simplify.}$$

Exercises for Example 1

Simplify the expression.

1. $\dfrac{5}{4x} + \dfrac{2}{4x}$

2. $\dfrac{3x}{10} + \dfrac{4x}{10}$

3. $\dfrac{4x + 1}{3x + 2} + \dfrac{x - 3}{3x + 2}$

Practice with Examples

For use with pages 658–662

EXAMPLE 2 *Subtract Rational Expressions*

Simplify $\dfrac{9}{x-1} - \dfrac{x+9}{x-1}$.

SOLUTION

$$\frac{9}{x-1} - \frac{x+9}{x-1} = \frac{9-(x+9)}{x+1}$$ Subtract the numerators.

$$= \frac{9-x-9}{x+1}$$ Distribute the negative.

$$= -\frac{x}{x+1}$$ Simplify.

Exercises for Example 2

Simplify the expression.

4. $\dfrac{6}{x+3} - \dfrac{4}{x+3}$

5. $\dfrac{7x}{2x+1} - \dfrac{6x-6}{2x+1}$

Practice with Examples

For use with pages 658–662

EXAMPLE 3 *Simplify after Subtracting*

Simplify $\dfrac{5x}{2x^2 + x - 1} - \dfrac{3x + 1}{2x^2 + x - 1}$.

SOLUTION

$$\dfrac{5x}{2x^2 + x - 1} - \dfrac{3x + 1}{2x^2 + x - 1} = \dfrac{5x - (3x + 1)}{2x^2 + x - 1} \quad \text{Subtract numerators.}$$

$$= \dfrac{2x - 1}{2x^2 + x - 1} \quad \text{Simplify.}$$

$$= \dfrac{2x - 1}{(2x - 1)(x + 1)} \quad \text{Factor.}$$

$$= \dfrac{\cancel{2x - 1}}{(\cancel{2x - 1})(x + 1)} \quad \text{Divide out common factor.}$$

$$= \dfrac{1}{x + 1} \quad \text{Simplify.}$$

Exercises for Example 3

Simplify the expression.

6. $\dfrac{2x}{x^2 + 5x + 6} - \dfrac{x - 2}{x^2 + 5x + 6}$

7. $\dfrac{x}{x^2 - 16} - \dfrac{4}{x^2 - 16}$

Practice with Examples

For use with pages 663–669

GOAL **Add and subtract rational expressions with unlike denominators.**

VOCABULARY

The least common multiple of unlike denominators is called the **least common denominator**, or **LCD**.

EXAMPLE 1 *Find the LCD of Rational Expressions*

Find the least common denominator of $\dfrac{7}{15x^2}$ and $\dfrac{x-3}{20x^3}$.

SOLUTION

$\begin{aligned}15x^2 &= 3 \cdot 5 \cdot x^2 \\ 20x^3 &= 2^2 \cdot 5 \cdot x^3\end{aligned}$ Factor the denominators.

$2^2,\ 3,\ 5,\ x^3$ Find the highest power of each factor.

$2^2 \cdot 3 \cdot 5 \cdot x^3 = 60x^3$ Multiply to find the LCD.

Exercises for Example 1

Find the least common denominator.

1. $\dfrac{x+3}{4}, \dfrac{5x}{6}$

2. $\dfrac{8}{9x^2}, \dfrac{2x+1}{12x}$

Practice with Examples

For use with pages 663–669

EXAMPLE 2 *Add Expressions with Unlike Denominators*

Simplify $\dfrac{3}{4x} + \dfrac{5}{6x^2}$.

SOLUTION

The LCD contains the highest power of each factor that appears in either denominator, so the LCD is $2^2 \cdot 3 \cdot x^2$, or $12x^2$.

$$\frac{3}{4x} + \frac{5}{6x^2} = \frac{3 \cdot 3x}{4x \cdot 3x} + \frac{5 \cdot 2}{6x^2 \cdot 2} \quad \text{Rewrite fractions using LCD.}$$

$$= \frac{9x}{12x^2} + \frac{10}{12x^2} \qquad \text{Simplify numerators and denominators.}$$

$$= \frac{9x + 10}{12x^2} \qquad \text{Add fractions.}$$

Exercises for Example 2

Simplify the expression.

3. $\dfrac{3}{5x} + \dfrac{2}{7x}$

4. $\dfrac{4}{x + 1} + \dfrac{5}{x + 2}$

5. $\dfrac{3x}{x + 4} + \dfrac{1}{2x + 8}$

Practice with Examples

For use with pages 663–669

EXAMPLE 3 *Subtract Expressions with Unlike Denominators*

Simplify $\dfrac{x}{x + 2} - \dfrac{3}{x - 3}$.

SOLUTION

The least common denominator is the product $(x + 2)(x - 3)$.

$$\dfrac{x}{x + 2} - \dfrac{3}{x - 3} = \dfrac{x(x - 3)}{(x + 2)(x - 3)} - \dfrac{3(x + 2)}{(x + 2)(x - 3)}$$ Rewrite fractions using LCD.

$$= \dfrac{x^2 - 3x}{(x + 2)(x - 3)} - \dfrac{3x + 6}{(x + 2)(x - 3)}$$ Simplify numerators. Leave denominators in factored form.

$$= \dfrac{x^2 - 3x - (3x + 6)}{(x + 2)(x - 3)}$$ Subtract fractions.

$$= \dfrac{x^2 - 3x - 3x - 6}{(x + 2)(x - 3)}$$ Use the distributive property.

$$= \dfrac{x^2 - 6x - 6}{(x + 2)(x - 3)}$$ Simplify.

Exercises for Example 3

Simplify the expression.

6. $\dfrac{x + 1}{x^2} - \dfrac{2}{3x}$

7. $\dfrac{2}{x + 1} - \dfrac{3}{x + 3}$

8. $\dfrac{3x}{x^2 + 2x} - \dfrac{4}{x + 2}$

Algebra 1, Concepts and Skills
Practice Workbook with Examples

Practice with Examples

For use with pages 670–677

GOAL Solve rational equations.

> **VOCABULARY**
>
> A **rational equation** is an equation that contains rational expressions.

EXAMPLE 1 *Cross Multiply*

Solve $\dfrac{2}{x} = \dfrac{x+2}{4}$.

SOLUTION

$\dfrac{2}{x} = \dfrac{x+2}{4}$	Write original equation.
$2(4) = x(x+2)$	Cross multiply.
$8 = x^2 + 2x$	Simplify.
$0 = x^2 + 2x - 8$	Write in standard form.
$0 = (x+4)(x-2)$	Factor right side.

If you set each factor equal to 0, the solutions are -4 and 2.

Exercises for Example 1

Solve the equation by cross multiplying.

1. $\dfrac{5}{w-3} = \dfrac{w}{2}$

2. $\dfrac{6}{x+1} = \dfrac{4}{x+2}$

3. $\dfrac{t}{9} = \dfrac{2}{t-3}$

Practice with Examples

For use with pages 670–677

EXAMPLE 2 *Factor First, Then Multiply by the LCD*

Solve $\dfrac{1}{x-2} + 1 = \dfrac{8}{x^2 - 5x + 6}$.

SOLUTION

The denominator $x^2 - 5x + 6$ factors as $(x-2)(x-3)$, so the LCD is $(x-2)(x-3)$. Multiply each side of the equation by $(x-2)(x-3)$.

$$\frac{1}{x-2} \cdot (x-2)(x-3) + 1 \cdot (x-2)(x-3) = \frac{8}{(x-2)(x-3)} \cdot (x-2)(x-3)$$

$$\frac{1(x-2)(x-3)}{x-2} + (x-2)(x-3) = \frac{8(x-2)(x-3)}{(x-2)(x-3)}$$

$$x - 3 + x^2 - 5x + 6 = 8$$

$$x^2 - 4x + 3 = 8$$

$$x^2 - 4x - 5 = 0$$

$$(x-5)(x+1) = 0$$

The solutions are 5 and -1. Check both values.

Exercises for Example 2

Solve the equation by multiplying by the least common denominator.

4. $\dfrac{1}{2x-10} - \dfrac{2}{x-5} = \dfrac{3}{4}$

5. $\dfrac{11}{x^2-16} = \dfrac{x}{x+4} - 2$

Algebra 1, Concepts and Skills
Practice Workbook with Examples

NAME _____ DATE _____

Practice with Examples

For use with pages 670–677

EXAMPLE 3 *Solve a Coin Problem*

Coins You have 8 coins worth $1.20. If you have only quarters and nickels, how many of each do you have?

SOLUTION

Let x = number of quarters.

Then $8 - x$ = number of nickels.

	Number	*Worth of coin*	*Value*
Quarters	x	0.25	$0.25x$
Nickels	$8 - x$	0.05	$0.05(8 - x)$

Verbal Model

$$\boxed{\begin{array}{c}\text{Value of}\\\text{quarters}\end{array}} + \boxed{\begin{array}{c}\text{Value of}\\\text{nickels}\end{array}} = \$1.20$$

Algebraic Model

$0.25x + 0.05(8 - x) = 1.20$	Write algebraic model.
$0.25x + 0.4 - 0.05x = 1.20$	Use distributive property
$25x + 40 - 5x = 120$	Multiply by 100.
$20x = 80$	Combine like terms.
$x = 4$	Divide each side by 20.
$8 - x = 4$	

Answer   You have 4 quarters and 4 nickels.

Exercises for Example 3

6. You have 12 coins worth $5.50. If you have only quarters and half-dollars, how many of each do you have?

Practice with Examples

For use with pages 691–697

GOAL Evaluate and graph a function involving square roots.

VOCABULARY

A **square-root function** is a function defined by the equation $y = \sqrt{x}$.

EXAMPLE 1 *Graphing* $y = a\sqrt{x} + k$

Find the domain of $y = 3\sqrt{x} + 2$. Then sketch its graph and find the range.

SOLUTION

The domain is the set of all nonnegative real numbers. Make a table of values, plot the points, and connect them with a smooth curve.

x	y
0	$y = 3\sqrt{0} + 2 = 2$
1	$y = 3\sqrt{1} + 2 = 5$
2	$y = 3\sqrt{2} + 2 \approx 6.2$
3	$y = 3\sqrt{3} + 2 \approx 7.2$
4	$y = 3\sqrt{4} + 2 = 8$

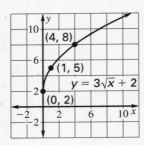

The range is the set of all real numbers that are greater than or equal to 2.

Exercises for Example 1

Find the domain of the function. Then sketch the graph and find the range.

1. $y = 2\sqrt{x} + 1$ **2.** $y = 2\sqrt{x} - 1$ **3.** $y = 2\sqrt{x} - 2$

NAME _____ DATE _____

Practice with Examples
For use with pages 691–697

EXAMPLE 2 **Graphing** $y = \sqrt{x - h}$

Find the domain of $y = \sqrt{x - 2}$. Then sketch its graph and find the range.

SOLUTION

To find the domain, find the values of x for which the radicand is nonnegative.

$\quad x - 2 \neq 0$ Write an inequality for the domain.

$\quad x \neq 2$ Add two to each side.

The domain is the set of all real numbers that are greater than or equal to 2.
Make a table of values, plot the points, and connect them with a smooth curve.

x	y
2	$y = \sqrt{2 - 2} = 0$
3	$y = \sqrt{3 - 2} = 1$
4	$y = \sqrt{4 - 2} \approx 1.4$
5	$y = \sqrt{5 - 2} \approx 1.7$
6	$y = \sqrt{6 - 2} = 2$

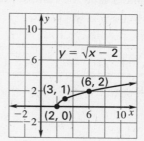

The range is the set of all nonnegative real numbers.

Exercises for Example 2

Find the domain of the function. Then sketch its graph and find the range.

4. $y = \sqrt{x - 1}$ **5.** $y = \sqrt{x + 1}$ **6.** $y = \sqrt{x - 4}$

NAME _____ DATE _____

Practice with Examples

For use with pages 691–697

EXAMPLE 3 *Using a Square-Root Model*

An object has been dropped from a height of h feet. The speed
S (in ft/sec) of the object right before it strikes the ground is
given by the model $S = \sqrt{64h}$.

a. Sketch the graph of the model.

b. Find the speed S (in ft/sec) of an object that has been
dropped from a height of 25 feet.

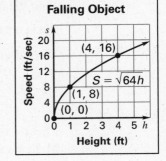

Falling Object

SOLUTION

a. Make a table of values, plot the points, and connect them
with a smooth curve.

h	0	1	2	3	4
S	$\sqrt{64 \cdot 0} = 0$	$\sqrt{64 \cdot 1} = 8$	$\sqrt{64 \cdot 2} \approx 11.3$	$\sqrt{64 \cdot 3} \approx 13.9$	$\sqrt{64 \cdot 4} = 16$

b. Substitute $h = 25$ into the model: $S = \sqrt{64 \cdot 25} = 40$ ft/sec

Exercise for Example 3

7. Use the model in Example 3 to find the speed S (in ft/sec) of
an object that has been dropped from a height of 36 feet.

Algebra 1, Concepts and Skills
Practice Workbook with Examples

Practice with Examples

For use with pages 698–703

GOAL Add, subtract, multiply, and divide radical expressions

EXAMPLE 1 *Adding and Subtracting Radicals*

Simplify the expression
$\sqrt{12} + \sqrt{3}$.

SOLUTION

$$\sqrt{12} + \sqrt{3} = \sqrt{4 \cdot 3} + \sqrt{3} \qquad \text{Perfect square factor}$$
$$= \sqrt{4} \cdot \sqrt{3} + \sqrt{3} \qquad \text{Use product property.}$$
$$= 2\sqrt{3} + \sqrt{3} \qquad \text{Simplify.}$$
$$= 3\sqrt{3} \qquad \text{Add radicals having same radicand.}$$

Exercises for Example 1

Simplify the expression.

1. $\sqrt{7} + 3\sqrt{7}$ **2.** $\sqrt{8} - \sqrt{2}$ **3.** $\sqrt{48} + \sqrt{3}$

EXAMPLE 2 *Multiplying Radicals*

Simplify the expression.

a. $\sqrt{3} \cdot \sqrt{12}$ **b.** $\sqrt{5}(\sqrt{2} + \sqrt{3})$ **c.** $(3 + \sqrt{2})(3 - \sqrt{2})$

SOLUTION

a. $\sqrt{3} \cdot \sqrt{12} = \sqrt{36}$ \qquad Use product property.

$\qquad\qquad = 6$ \qquad Simplify.

b. $\sqrt{5}(\sqrt{2} + \sqrt{3}) = \sqrt{5} \cdot \sqrt{2} + \sqrt{5} \cdot \sqrt{3}$ \qquad Use distributive property.

$\qquad\qquad\qquad = \sqrt{10} + \sqrt{15}$ \qquad Use product property.

c. $(3 + \sqrt{2})(3 - \sqrt{2}) = 3^2 - (\sqrt{2})^2$ \qquad Use sum and difference pattern.

$\qquad\qquad\qquad = 9 - 2 = 7$ \qquad Simplify.

Practice with Examples

For use with pages 698–703

Exercises for Example 2

Simplify the expression.

4. $\left(\sqrt{2} + 1\right)\left(\sqrt{2} - 1\right)$

5. $\sqrt{3} \cdot \sqrt{6}$

6. $\sqrt{10}\left(2 + \sqrt{2}\right)$

EXAMPLE 3 *Simplifying Radicals*

Simplify $\dfrac{5}{\sqrt{2}}$.

SOLUTION

$$\frac{5}{\sqrt{2}} = \frac{5}{\sqrt{2}} \cdot \frac{\sqrt{2}}{\sqrt{2}} \qquad \text{Multiply numerator and denominator by } \sqrt{2}.$$

$$= \frac{5\sqrt{2}}{\sqrt{2} \cdot \sqrt{2}} \qquad \text{Multiply fractions.}$$

$$= \frac{5\sqrt{2}}{2} \qquad \text{Simplify.}$$

Exercises for Example 3

Simplify the expression.

7. $\dfrac{4}{\sqrt{3}}$

8. $\dfrac{5}{\sqrt{8}}$

9. $\dfrac{-1}{\sqrt{12}}$

NAME _____ DATE _____

Practice with Examples
For use with pages 698–703

EXAMPLE 4 *Using a Radical Model*

A tsunami is an enormous ocean wave that can be caused by underwater earthquakes, volcanic eruptions, or hurricanes. The speed S of a tsunami in miles per hour is given by the model $S = 3.86\sqrt{d}$ where d is the depth of the ocean in feet. Suppose one tsunami is at a depth of 1792 feet and another is at a depth of 1372 feet. Write an expression that represents the difference in speed between the tsunamis. Simplify the expression.

SOLUTION

The speed of the first tsunami mentioned is $3.86\sqrt{1792}$ while the speed of the second tsunami is $3.86\sqrt{1372}$. The difference D between the speeds can be represented by $3.86\sqrt{1792} - 3.86\sqrt{1372}$.

$$\begin{aligned} D &= 3.86\sqrt{1792} - 3.86\sqrt{1372} \\ &= 3.86\sqrt{7 \cdot 256} - 3.86\sqrt{7 \cdot 196} \\ &= 61.76\sqrt{7} - 54.04\sqrt{7} = 7.72\sqrt{7} \end{aligned}$$

Exercise for Example 4

10. Rework Example 4 if one tsunami is at a depth of 3125 feet and another tsunami is at a depth of 2000 feet.

Practice with Examples

For use with pages 704–709

GOAL **Solve a radical equation.**

EXAMPLE 1 *Solving a Radical Equation*

Solve $\sqrt{3x + 1} + 2 = 6$.

SOLUTION

Isolate the radical expression on one side of the equation.

$\sqrt{3x + 1} + 2 = 6$ Write original equation.

$\sqrt{3x + 1} = 4$ Subtract 2 from each side.

$\left(\sqrt{3x + 1}\right)^2 = 4^2$ Square each side.

$3x + 1 = 16$ Simplify.

$3x = 15$ Subtract 1 from each side.

$x = 5$ Divide each side by 3.

The solution is 5. Check the solution in the original equation.

Exercises for Example 1

Solve the equation.

1. $\sqrt{x + 2} = 3$ **2.** $\sqrt{x} + 2 = 3$ **3.** $\sqrt{4x + 1} = 3$

Algebra 1, Concepts and Skills
Practice Workbook with Examples

NAME _____ DATE _____

Practice with Examples
For use with pages 704–709

EXAMPLE 2 *Checking for Extraneous Solutions*

Solve the equation $\sqrt{2x + 3} = x$ and check for extraneous solutions.

SOLUTION

$\sqrt{2x + 3} = x$	Write original equation.
$(\sqrt{2x + 3})^2 = x^2$	Square each side.
$2x + 3 = x^2$	Simplify.
$0 = x^2 - 2x - 3$	Write in standard form.
$0 = (x - 3)(x + 1)$	Factor.
$x = 3$ or $x = -1$	Use zero-product property.

To check the solutions, substitute 3 and -1 in the original equation.

$$\sqrt{2(3) + 3} \stackrel{?}{=} 3 \qquad\qquad \sqrt{2(-1) + 3} \stackrel{?}{=} -1$$

$$\sqrt{9} \stackrel{?}{=} 3 \qquad\qquad\qquad \sqrt{1} \stackrel{?}{=} -1$$

$$3 = 3 \qquad\qquad\qquad\quad 1 \neq -1$$

The only solution is 3, because $x = -1$ is not a solution.

Exercises for Example 2

Solve the equation and check for extraneous solutions.

4. $\sqrt{x + 2} = x$ **5.** $\sqrt{3x} + 6 = 0$ **6.** $\sqrt{x + 6} = x$

Practice with Examples

For use with pages 704–709

EXAMPLE 3 *Using a Radical Model*

The distance d (in centimeters) that tap water is absorbed up a strip of blotting paper at a temperature of 28.4°C is given by the model $d = 0.444\sqrt{t}$, where t is the time (in seconds). Approximately how many minutes would it take for the water to travel a distance of 16 centimeters up the strip of blotting paper?

SOLUTION

$d = 0.444\sqrt{t}$	Write model for blotting paper distance.
$16 = 0.444\sqrt{t}$	Substitute 16 for d.
$\dfrac{16}{0.444} = \sqrt{t}$	Divide each side by 0.444.
$\left(\dfrac{16}{0.444}\right)^2 = t$	Square each side.
$1299 \approx t$	Simplify.

It would take approximately 1299 seconds for the water to travel a distance of 16 centimeters up the strip of blotting paper. To find the time in minutes, you divide 1299 by 60. It would take approximately 22 minutes.

Exercises for Example 3

7. Use the model in Example 3 to find the distance that the water would travel in 36 seconds.

8. Use the model in Example 3 to find the number of seconds that it would take for the water to travel a distance of 10 centimeters up the strip of blotting paper.

Algebra 1, Concepts and Skills
Practice Workbook with Examples

NAME _____ DATE _____

Practice with Examples

For use with pages 710–715

GOAL Evaluate expressions involving rational exponents.

EXAMPLE 1 *Finding Cube and Square Roots*

Just as squaring a number is the inverse of finding the square root of that number, the inverse of cubing a number is finding the **cube root**. You can use rational exponents to write square roots and cube rots.

square root of a	cube root of a
$\sqrt{a} = a^{1/2}$	$\sqrt[3]{a} = a^{1/3}$

a. $125^{1/3}$ Because $5^3 = 125$, you know that $125^{1/3} = 5$.

b. $\sqrt[3]{64}$ Because $4^3 = 64$, you know that $\sqrt[3]{64} = 4$.

c. $25^{1/2}$ Because $5^2 = 25$, you know that $25^{1/2} = 5$.

Exercises for Example 1
....

Evaluate the expression without using a calculator.

1. $125^{1/2}$ **2.** $8^{1/3}$ **3.** $81^{1/2}$

4. $169^{1/2}$ **5.** $\sqrt[3]{216}$ **6.** $\sqrt[3]{1000}$

EXAMPLE 2 *Evaluating Expressions with Rational Exponents*

a. $25^{3/2} = (25^{1/2})^3$ Use power of a power property.

         $= (5)^3$ Find square root.

         $= 125$ Evaluate power.

     Another Way: $25^{3/2} = (\sqrt{25})^3$ Rewrite using radical notation.

             $= (5)^3$ The square root of 25 is 5.

             $= 125$ Evaluate power.

Practice with Examples

For use with pages 710–715

b. $216^{4/3} = (216^{1/3})^4$ Use power of a power property.

          $= (6)^4$ Find cube root.

          $= 1296$ Evaluate power.

Another way: $216^{4/3} = (\sqrt[3]{216})^4$ Rewrite using radical notation.

                 $= 6^4$ The cube root of 216 is 6.

                 $= 1296$ Evaluate power.

Exercises for Example 2

Evaluate the expression without using a calculator.

7. $8^{5/3}$ **8.** $9^{3/2}$ **9.** $64^{4/3}$

10. $125^{2/3}$ **11.** $81^{3/2}$ **12.** $1000^{4/3}$

EXAMPLE 3   *Using Properties of Rational Exponents*

a. $6^{1/2} \times 6^{3/2} = (6^{1/2 + 3/2})$ Use product of powers property.

              $= 6^{4/2} = 6^2 = 36$ Simplify.

b. $(11^{1/3})^9 = (11^{1/3 \times 9})$ Use power of a power property.

           $= (11^3)$ Simplify.

           $= 1331$ Simplify.

NAME _____ DATE _____

Practice with Examples

For use with pages 710–715

   c. $(16 \times 25)^{1/2} = 16^{1/2} \times 25^{1/2}$ Use power of a product property.

                $= 4 \times 5 = 20$ Simplify.

Exercises for Example 3

Evaluate using the properties of rational exponents.

13. $(4^3)^{1/3}$ **14.** $(8 \cdot 27)^{1/3}$ **15.** $16^{1/2} \cdot 36^{1/2}$

16. $(3^6)^{2/3}$ **17.** $9^{5/2} \cdot 9^{1/2}$ **18.** $(16^{3/2})^{1/2}$

EXAMPLE 4   Using Properties of Rational Exponents

   Simplify the variable expression $(x \cdot y^{3/2})^4 x$.

        $(x \cdot y^{3/2})^4 x = (x^4 \cdot y^{3/2 \cdot 4})x$ Rewrite using the power of a product property.

                $= x^4 \cdot y^6 \cdot x$ Simplify.

                $= x^{4+1} \cdot y^6$ Use product of powers property.

                $= x^5 \cdot y^6$ Simplify.

Exercises for Example 4

Simplify the expression.

19. $(x^2 \cdot y)^{1/2}$ **20.** $(y^4)^{1/8}$ **21.** $(x^{3/4} \cdot x^{1/4})^2$

22. $(y^6)^{1/3}$ **23.** $(x^{1/2} \cdot y)^4 x$ **24.** $\sqrt[3]{x}(x^6 \cdot y^2)^{1/3}$

NAME _____ DATE _____

Practice with Examples

For use with pages 715–721

GOAL Solve a quadratic equation by completing the square.

VOCABULARY

To **complete the square** of the expression $x^2 + bx$, add the square of half the coefficient of x.

$$x^2 + bx + \left(\frac{b}{2}\right)^2 = \left(x + \frac{b}{2}\right)^2$$

EXAMPLE 1 *Completing the Square*

Solve $x^2 - 18x + 5 = 0$ by completing the square.

SOLUTION

$x^2 - 18x + 5 = 0$	Write original equation.
$x^2 - 18x = -5$	Subtract 5 from each side.
$x^2 - 18x + \left(\frac{18}{2}\right)^2 = -5 + 81$	Add $\left(\frac{18}{2}\right)^2$, or 81 to each side.
$(x - 9)^2 = 76$	Write left side as perfect square.
$x - 9 = \pm\sqrt{76}$	Find square root of each side.
$x = 9 \pm 2\sqrt{19}$	Add 9 to each side.

The solutions are $9 + 2\sqrt{19}$ and $9 - 2\sqrt{19}$. Both solutions check in the original equation.

Exercises for Example 1

Solve the equation by completing the square.

1. $n^2 - 3n = 2$ **2.** $y^2 + 4y = -1$ **3.** $b^2 + 8b + 3 = 0$

Algebra 1, Concepts and Skills
Practice Workbook with Examples

Practice with Examples

For use with pages 715–721

EXAMPLE 2 *Choosing a Solution Method*

Choose a method to solve the quadratic equation.

  a. $5x^2 + 3x - 2 = 0$ **b.** $x^2 + 6x - 1 = 0$

SOLUTION

  a. This equation can be factored easily.

$5x^2 + 3x - 2 = 0$	Write original equation.
$(5x - 2)(x + 1) = 0$	Factor.
$5x - 2 = 0$ or $x + 1 = 0$	Zero-product property
$x = \dfrac{2}{5}$ or $x = -1$	Solve for x.

The solutions are $\dfrac{2}{5}$ and -1.

  b. This equation cannot be solved by factoring, but it can be solved by
     completing the square.

$x^2 + 6x - 1 = 0$	Write original equation.
$x^2 + 6x = 1$	Add 1 to each side.
$x^2 + 6x + \left(\dfrac{6}{2}\right)^2 = 1 + 9$	Add $\left(\dfrac{6}{2}\right)^2$, or 9 to each side.
$(x + 3)^2 = 10$	Write left side as perfect square.
$x + 3 = \pm\sqrt{10}$	Find square root of each side.
$x = -3 \pm \sqrt{10}$	Subtract 3 from each side.

The solutions are $-3 + \sqrt{10}$ and $-3 - \sqrt{10}$.

Practice with Examples

For use with pages 715–721

Exercises for Example 2

Choose a method to solve the quadratic equation. Explain your choice.

4. $5y^2 - 35 = 0$

5. $w^2 - 3w - 10 = 0$

6. $x^2 + 4x - 7 = 0$

Algebra 1, Concepts and Skills
Practice Workbook with Examples

NAME _____ DATE _____

Practice with Examples

For use with pages 722–729

GOAL   **Use the Pythagorean theorem and its converse.**

VOCABULARY

In a right triangle, the **hypotenuse** is the side opposite the right angle; the other two sides are the **legs.**

The **Pythagorean theorem** states that if a triangle is a right triangle, then the sum of the squares of the lengths of the legs a and b equals the square of the length of the hypotenuse c, or $a^2 + b^2 = c^2$.

In a statement of the form "If p, then q," p is the *hypothesis* and q is the *conclusion.* The **converse** of the statement "If p, then q" is the related statement "If q, then p."

The **converse of the Pythagorean theorem** states that if a triangle has side lengths a, b, and c such that $a^2 + b^2 = c^2$, then the triangle is a right triangle.

EXAMPLE 1   *Using the Pythagorean Theorem*

A right triangle has one leg that is 1 inch longer than the other leg. The hypotenuse is 5 inches. Find the lengths of the legs.

SOLUTION

Sketch a right triangle and label the sides. Let x be the length of the shorter leg. Use the Pythagorean theorem to solve for x.

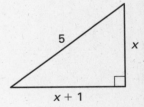

$a^2 + b^2 = c^2$	Write Pythagorean theorem.
$x^2 + (x + 1)^2 = 5^2$	Substitute for a, b, and c.
$x^2 + x^2 + 2x + 1 = 25$	Simplify.
$2x^2 + 2x - 24 = 0$	Write in standard form.
$2(x + 4)(x - 3) = 0$	Factor.
$x = -4 \text{ or } x = 3$	Zero-product property

Length is positive, so the solution $x = -4$ is extraneous. The sides have lengths 3 inches and $3 + 1 = 4$ inches.

Algebra 1, Concepts and Skills
Practice Workbook with Examples

NAME _____ DATE _____

Practice with Examples

For use with pages 722–729

Exercises for Example 1

Use the Pythagorean theorem to find the missing length of the right triangle.

1.

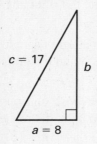

$c = 17$
b
$a = 8$

2.

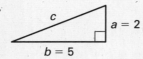

c
$a = 2$
$b = 5$

3.

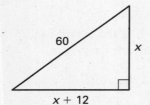

60
x
$x + 12$

Algebra 1, Concepts and Skills
Practice Workbook with Examples

NAME _____ DATE _____

Practice with Examples

For use with pages 722–729

EXAMPLE 2 *Determining Right Triangles*

Determine whether the given lengths are sides of a right triangle.

  a. 12, 16, 20   **b.** 10, 24, 25

SOLUTION

Use the converse of the Pythagorean theorem.

  a. The lengths are sides of a right triangle because

$$12^2 + 16^2 = 144 + 256 = 400 = 20^2.$$

  b. The lengths are not sides of a right triangle because

$$10^2 + 24^2 = 100 + 576 = 676 \neq 25^2.$$

Exercises for Example 2

Determine whether the given lengths are sides of a right triangle.

  4. 8, 15, 17

  5. 3, 6, 7

  6. 9, 40, 41

NAME _____ DATE _____

Practice with Examples

For use with pages 730–735

GOAL Find the distance between two points in a coordinate plane.

EXAMPLE 1 *Finding the Distance Between Two Points*

Find the distance between $(-1, 2)$ and $(3, 7)$ using the distance formula.

SOLUTION

$$d = \sqrt{(x_2 - x_1)^2 + (y_2 - y_1)^2} \qquad \text{Write distance formula.}$$
$$ = \sqrt{(-1 - 3)^2 + (2 - 7)^2} \qquad \text{Substitute.}$$
$$ = \sqrt{41} \qquad \text{Simplify.}$$
$$ \approx 6.40 \qquad \text{Use a calculator.}$$

Exercises for Example 1

Find the distance between the two points. Round the result to the nearest hundredth if necessary.

1. $(0, 4), (-3, 0)$

2. $(2, 3), (4, 5)$

3. $(-4, 2), (1, 4)$

Algebra 1, Concepts and Skills
Practice Workbook with Examples

Practice with Examples

For use with pages 730–735

EXAMPLE 2 *Checking a Right Triangle*

Determine whether the points $(4, 6)$, $(2, 1)$, and $(-2, 3)$ are vertices of a right triangle.

SOLUTION

Use the distance formula to find the lengths of the three sides.

$d_1 = \sqrt{(4 - 2)^2 + (6 - 1)^2} = \sqrt{2^2 + 5^2} = \sqrt{4 + 25} = \sqrt{29}$

$d_2 = \sqrt{[4 - (-2)]^2 + (6 - 3)^2} = \sqrt{6^2 + 3^2} = \sqrt{36 + 9} = \sqrt{45}$

$d_3 = \sqrt{[2 - (-2)]^2 + (1 - 3)^2} = \sqrt{4^2 + (-2)^2} = \sqrt{16 + 4} = \sqrt{20}$

Find the sum of the squares of the lengths of the two shorter sides.

$$d_1{}^2 + d_3{}^2 = (\sqrt{29})^2 + (\sqrt{20})^2$$
$$= 29 + 20$$
$$= 49$$

The sum of the squares of the lengths of the two shorter sides is 49, which is not equal to the square of the longest side, $(\sqrt{45})^2$. By the converse of the Pythagorean Theorem, the given points are not the vertices of a right triangle.

Exercise for Example 2

4. Determine whether $(3, 7)$, $(6, 2)$, and $(-1, -2)$ are vertices of a right triangle. Explain your answer.

Practice with Examples

For use with pages 730–735

EXAMPLE 3 *Applying the Distance Formula*

From your home, you ride your bicycle 5 miles north, then 12 miles east. How far are you from your home?

SOLUTION

You can superimpose a coordinate system on a diagram of your bicycle trip. You start at the point $(0, 0)$ and finish at the point $(12, 5)$. Use the distance formula.

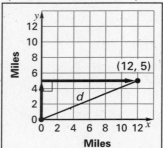

$$d = \sqrt{(12 - 0)^2 + (5 - 0)^2}$$
$$= \sqrt{144 + 25}$$
$$= \sqrt{169}$$
$$= 13$$

You are 13 miles from your home.

Exercise for Example 3

5. Rework Example 3 if you ride 8 miles east and 15 miles south.

LESSON 12.8

Practice with Examples

For use with pages 736–739

GOAL Find the midpoint of a line segment in a coordinate plane

---

VOCABULARY

The **midpoint** of a line segment is the point on the segment that is equidistant from its endpoints.

EXAMPLE 1 *Finding the Midpoint*

Find the midpoint of the line segment connecting the points $(-8, -4)$ and $(2, 0)$.

SOLUTION

Use the midpoint formula for the points (x_1, y_1) and (x_2, y_2): $\left(\dfrac{x_1 + x_2}{2}, \dfrac{y_1 + y_2}{2} \right)$.

$$\left(\frac{-8 + 2}{2}, \frac{-4 + 0}{2} \right) = \left(\frac{-6}{2}, \frac{-4}{2} \right) = (-3, -2)$$

The midpoint is $(-3, -2)$.

Exercises for Example 1

Find the midpoint of the line segment connecting the given points.

1. $(1, 3), (4, 5)$

2. $(6, 1), (-4, -1)$

3. $(6, 0), (0, 2)$

Algebra 1, Concepts and Skills
Practice Workbook with Examples

NAME _____ DATE _____

Practice with Examples

For use with pages 736–739

EXAMPLE 2 *Checking a Midpoint*

Use the distance formula to check the midpoint in Example 1.

SOLUTION

The distance between $(-3, -2)$ and $(-8, -4)$ is

$$d_1 = \sqrt{[-3 - (-8)]^2 + [-2 - (-4)]^2} = \sqrt{5^2 + 2^2} = \sqrt{25 + 4} = \sqrt{29}.$$

The distance between $(-3, -2)$ and $(2, 0)$ is

$$d_2 = \sqrt{(-3 - 2)^2 + (-2 - 0)^2} = \sqrt{(-5)^2 + (-2)^2} = \sqrt{25 + 4} = \sqrt{29}.$$

The distances from $(-3, -2)$ to the ends of the segment are equal.

Exercises for Example 2

4–6. Show that the midpoints found in Exercises 1–3 are the same distance from each point.

Algebra 1, Concepts and Skills
Practice Workbook with Examples

NAME _____ DATE _____

Practice with Examples

For use with pages 736–739

EXAMPLE 3 *Applying the Midpoint Formula*

You and a friend agree to meet halfway between your two towns, as shown on the graph at the right. Find the location where you should meet.

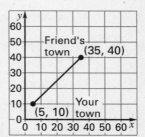

SOLUTION

The coordinates of your town are (5, 10) and the coordinates of your friend's town are (35, 40). Use the midpoint formula to find the point that is halfway between the two towns.

$$\left(\frac{5 + 35}{2}, \frac{10 + 40}{2}\right) = \left(\frac{40}{2}, \frac{50}{2}\right)$$

$$= (20, 25)$$

You should meet at (20, 25).

Exercise for Example 3

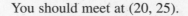

7. Rework Example 3 if the coordinates of your town are (0, 35) and the coordinates of your friend's town are (30, 15).

Practice with Examples

For use with pages 740–746

GOAL **Use logical reasoning and proof to prove that a statement is true or false.**

> ### VOCABULARY
>
> **Postulates** or **axioms** are properties in mathematics that we accept to be true without proof.
>
> **Theorems** are statements that have to be proved.
>
> A **conjecture** is a statement that is believed to be true but not yet proved.
>
> In an **indirect proof,** or a *proof by contradiction,* you assume a statement is false. If this leads to an impossibility, then the original statement is true.

EXAMPLE 1 *Proving a Theorem*

Prove the cancellation property of addition: If $a + c = b + c$, then $a = b$.

SOLUTION

$a + c = b + c$	Write original property.
$a + c + (-c) = b + c + (-c)$	Addition property of equality
$a + [c + (-c)] = b + [c + (-c)]$	Associative property of addition
$a + 0 = b + 0$	Inverse property of addition
$a = b$	Identity property of addition

Exercises for Example 1
Prove the theorem using the basic axioms of algebra.

1. If $ac = bc$, then $a = b$, $c \neq 0$.

2. If $a - c = b - c$, then $a = b$.

Practice with Examples

For use with pages 740–746

EXAMPLE 2 *Finding a Counterexample*

Assign values to a and b to show that the rule $\dfrac{1}{a + b} = \dfrac{1}{a} + \dfrac{1}{b}$ is false.

SOLUTION

You can choose any values of a and b, except $a = -b$, $a = 0$, or $b = 0$.
Let $a = 3$ and $b = 1$. Evaluate the left side of the equation.

$$\dfrac{1}{a + b} = \dfrac{1}{3 + 1} \qquad \text{Substitute 3 for } a \text{ and 1 for } b.$$

$$= \dfrac{1}{4} \qquad \text{Simplify.}$$

Evaluate the right side of the equation.

$$\dfrac{1}{a} + \dfrac{1}{b} = \dfrac{1}{3} + \dfrac{1}{1} \qquad \text{Substitute 3 for } a \text{ and 1 for } b.$$

$$= \dfrac{4}{3} \qquad \text{Simplify.}$$

Because $\dfrac{1}{4} \neq \dfrac{4}{3}$, you have shown one case in which the rule is false.

The counterexample of $a = 3$ and $b = 1$ is sufficient to prove that
$\dfrac{1}{a + b} = \dfrac{1}{a} + \dfrac{1}{b}$ is false.

Exercises for Example 2

Find a counterexample to show that the statement is not true.

3. $\sqrt{a^2 + b^2} = a + b$ **4.** $a - b = b - a$ **5.** $a \div b = b \div a$

Practice with Examples

For use with pages 740–746

EXAMPLE 3 *Using an Indirect Proof*

Use an indirect proof to prove the conclusion is true:

If $\dfrac{a}{b} \neq \dfrac{c}{b}$ and $b > 0$, then $a \neq c$.

SOLUTION

Assume that $a \neq c$ is not true. Then $a < c$.

$a < c$	Assume the opposite of $a \neq c$ is true.
$\dfrac{a}{b} < \dfrac{c}{b}$	Dividing each side by the same positive number produces an equivalent inequality.

This contradicts the given statement that $\dfrac{a}{b} \neq \dfrac{c}{b}$. Therefore, it is impossible that $a < c$.

You conclude that $a \neq c$ is true.

Exercise for Example 3

6. Use an indirect proof to prove that the conclusion is true:
   If $a + b > b + c$, then $a > c$.

Algebra 1, Concepts and Skills
Practice Workbook with Examples